MICHELANGELO
DRAWINGS
PHAIDON PRESS

MICHELANGELO DRAWINGS

BY LUDWIG GOLDSCHEIDER

THE PHAIDON PRESS · LONDON

COPYRIGHT 1951 BY PHAIDON PRESS LTD · LONDON · SW7

MADE IN GREAT BRITAIN

PLATES PRINTED BY CLARKE & SHERWELL LTD · NORTHAMPTON

TEXT PRINTED BY TONBRIDGE PRINTERS LTD · TONBRIDGE

BOUND BY KEY & WHITING LTD · LONDON

BOOK DESIGNED BY THE AUTHOR

CONTENTS

FOREWORD

*The vulgar sort of infidell people which scarcely beleeve any
hearbe but such they see in their owne Gardens, or any knowledge
but such as is bred in their owne braines, or any birds which are
not hatched in their owne Nests . . .*

EDWARD TOPSELL, 1607

THIS VOLUME was conceived a long time ago on a much more problematic and less popular basis, namely, as a critical sifting of those drawings which in my opinion have been wrongly attributed to Michelangelo, and an attempt to define the work of his various imitators. Originally I intended to have separate chapters on Bacchiacca, Battista Franco, Tribolo, Taddeo Zuccaro, etc., but in the course of my studies it soon became evident that so many genuine drawings of Michelangelo's had been rejected by more recent critics, that the generally accepted criteria of attribution seemed to have vanished and had first to be restored.

In addition to this, there is still no complete corpus of Michelangelo drawings, and the quality of the reproductions leaves much to be desired. Even the costly collotype plates in Frey's publication were severely criticized by Berenson (Catalogue, 1938, pp. 160–161): 'Among the less trustworthy are the reproductions in Frey's indispensable work on Michelangelo. . . . Considering that most students, particularly in Germany, will base their studies on Frey's reproductions, they must be seriously warned that they seldom do justice to the originals, and that conclusions regarding the originals should not be derived from them. . . . The student should rely rather on the Alinari, Braun, Anderson and Brogi photographs. For the Louvre and the British Museum, Alinari's prints are particularly to be recommended.'[1]

Apart from the question of quality, the volumes of reproductions hitherto published are none of them complete. This is evident from the fact that the present selection contains forty reproductions which are not to be found in Frey's corpus and forty-five which are lacking in Berenson's volume of plates.[2] On the other hand, an almost complete catalogue of all Michelangelo's drawings is available to the student, provided he is willing to combine the catalogues of Frey, Thode, Berenson and Wilde, to which must be added the drawings in the Archivio Buonarroti and the Codex Vaticanus published by Tolnay.

Having thus altered my conception of the task, I have tried to give, by means of a selection, an intrinsically complete idea of all the phases and forms of Michelangelo's art

---

[1] On the other hand, I have found that all Braun's photographs, and some of Alinari's prints, show evidence of much retouching, while the available photographs of the drawings in the Louvre proved, when compared with the originals, to be so inadequate that I had to have most of them photographed again. New photographs had also to be made of many of the drawings in the British Museum, the Casa Buonarroti, the Uffizi, and at Haarlem, and I am grateful to the directors of these collections for enabling this to be done; and also to Brinsley Ford, Esq., who has generously allowed a new photograph to be taken of the fine drawing in his collection.

[2] The present volume might be of some value even to the specialist, as it contains several reproductions which are shown here for the first time. No. 75, a sketch for the Resurrected Christ, had remained unpublished hitherto; the similar drawings, Nos. 76 and 80, had, so far as I am aware, never before been published adequately, and the same applies to the Bayonne sketches for the Last Judgement, Nos. 98 and 99, the two figures for the second version of the Colonna Crucifixion, Nos. 115 and 116 (cf. Plate 137), and a few other drawings.

monument to Sforza, while Verrocchio, his former teacher, was busy in Venice in 1488 with the casting of his Colleoni monument, and died there in the same year. The new paintings which evoked the greatest admiration in Florence at this time were works of masters from the Low Countries—Rogier van der Weyden's 'Entombment' and Hugo van der Goes' Portinari triptych, together with a picture with a mysterious leaning towards the antique, Signorelli's 'Kingdom of Pan', which Lorenzo de' Medici brought to Florence from Cortona in this very year 1488.[2] Mythological works by Botticelli and Piero di Cosimo, painted at the same time, were closely akin to this masterpiece of Signorelli's. Filippino Lippi, a forerunner of the Mannerists, had received in the same year the commission for the frescoes in the Caraffa chapel at Rome, while Antonio Pollaiuolo and his brother were on the point of leaving for Rome to work there on the monuments of the two Popes. Except for Botticelli and Piero di Cosimo, Ghirlandaio was the only painter of any importance left in Florence. Like the worthy craftsman he was, he went on painting his spacious family portraits, his social pictures set in architectonic landscapes, which claimed to be religious paintings. Such was the man from whom Michelangelo was supposed to learn painting.

Under the patronage of the Medici and other merchant families, art in Florence had assumed an elegant, sophisticated character, pleasingly reminiscent of the antique, familiar and decorative—it became, in fact, an art of interior decoration. The best pictures of the period remind us of *cassoni*, even if they fill a whole wall; the best sculptures seem like portrait busts or small bronze statues that can be stood on tables. Only architecture retained its grand manner. It can hardly be supposed that among the pictures painted at that time Michelangelo found any that he held to be equal to the old frescoes of Giotto and Masaccio, which he copied. In his eyes even the plastic works of Andrea della Robbia and Antonio Pollaiuolo would not have seemed comparable to the works of Giovanni Pisano, Donatello and Ghiberti. An afterglow of Donatello's genius survived in the work of his assistant Bertoldo, whose pupil Michelangelo became.

Bertoldo's school was in the garden of the Casino Mediceo, and was under the patronage of Lorenzo de' Medici, who not only provided the salaries of the teachers, but also helped the pupils by paying them stipends, supplying them with rooms in his house, and allowing them to eat at his table. Michelangelo entered the Medici palace as a guest. Lorenzo, who was certainly not the worst poet nor the least able philosopher among the members of his Platonic Academy, also exercised an influence on Bertoldo's school. We are told that he criticized Michelangelo's first sculpture, the head of a faun. Poliziano, the shining light of the Academy, who provided Michelangelo with the subject-matter for his Centaur relief, seems in other ways, too, to have inspired the school with a humanistic spirit. For the rest, the pupils made drawings after the antique sculptures, gems and cameos preserved in the building, and after the cartoons and models of Donatello, Brunelleschi, Masaccio, Uccello and Fra Angelico—a collection of works which made of the Casino Mediceo a veritable museum. Brunelleschi and Uccello obviously supplied the models for the study of perspective; anatomy—which in those days meant the structure of muscles and the movements of the body—was studied with the aid of antique statues. In this school, too, Michelangelo passed over the earlier stages of study. Vasari relates how, soon after joining Bertoldo's school, Michelangelo was watching the young Torrigiano working on clay statuettes—'Michelangelo watched and then immediately began to form such statuettes'. In a later passage Vasari mentions Michelangelo's talent for overcoming all difficulties and the effortless ease with which he worked—'la maniera difficile con

---

[2] Vasari, ed. Milanesi, III, p. 689. A. Chastel, in *Journal of the Warburg Institute*, VIII, 1945, p. 66. R. Langton Douglas, *Piero di Cosimo*, 1946, p. 19.

facilissima facilità'—and this must have been due to the fact that the young artist made 'a close study of nature every day'.

By 'study of nature' we must understand naturalism—not merely a realistic observation and rendering of superficial phenomena, but a careful penetration of the structure and laws of all living things, and an experimenting with the optical possibilities which can lead to a perfect reproduction.

Whereas realism holds up before nature a flat and all too small mirror, in naturalism the human eye registers the forms of a phenomenon and then, with the aid of knowledge of their origins and functions, endows them with a magical element. The great naturalistic draughtsman of Florence, Leonardo, could render a tree in such a way that we seem to see its roots in the ground and to feel how its summit breathes the air; he drew strata of earth, and waves of water in such a way that we sense the pent-up power behind them.

It was this almost scientific penetration of nature that Michelangelo strove to achieve in his early days. We are told that he made a copy in colours of Schongauer's engraving of 'The Temptation of St. Anthony', but that before doing so he went to the market and bought some fish, in order that he might improve his copy by first studying the structure and colouring of the scales; and that, when he carved a Crucified Christ for the Prior of Santo Spirito, he had corpses sent from the hospital of the convent and dissected them.

For the rest, Michelangelo made drawings during this period at the Casino Mediceo (where Torrigiano, Granacci, Bugiardini and Montelupo were his fellow-pupils) after antique statues, and copied, as we have already mentioned, figures from the frescoes of Masaccio, whose monumental forms must have excited his admiration to the same degree that Ghirlandaio's petty realism left him unmoved.

In 1491, during Michelangelo's second year at the school, Bertoldo died, and that was the end of his apprenticeship.

We must consider what that meant. At the end of the fifteenth century, a time when the duration of apprenticeship, service as a journeyman, examination for mastership and admission to a guild were all strictly regulated, Michelangelo had had virtually no training. At the age of sixteen he was an accomplished young master who had already produced a number of original reliefs. Michelangelo was a self-taught man. Even if it can be affirmed that he learned the elements of painting and sculpture from his two masters and his fellow-pupils, it nevertheless remains a mystery how and where he acquired his knowledge of architecture, a subject incomparably more difficult.

Michelangelo's patron, Lorenzo de' Medici, died in 1492, Ghirlandaio and Poliziano in 1494; in the same year Charles VIII crossed the Alps and marched on Florence at the head of his army. The Medici were driven out of the city; Michelangelo fled to Bologna, then returned for a short time to Florence and afterwards went to Rome, where he began his second apprenticeship. Once again he was his own teacher.

He made drawings after antique sculptures, a good example of these being the drawing after an antique Putto and a Mercury (Plate 10).

In this essay I do not intend to follow Michelangelo's career in Italy, or to discuss all his works in connexion with my selection of his drawings. The Catalogue goes from year to year and from drawing to drawing, and contains in chronological order things that I do not intend to repeat here. In the preceding paragraphs I have endeavoured to explain the perspective in which I see Michelangelo's beginnings; in those which follow I shall try to render my survey schematic, in the same way as a map shows landscape—in other words, I wish merely to indicate the trends Michelangelo followed as a draughtsman and to mark the points at which his style underwent a change.[3]

---

[3] Psychologists might find it interesting to investigate how often in Michelangelo's life a break of style was preceded by a severe illness.

The first stylistic break occurred in 1501. In that year Michelangelo saw Leonardo's recently finished cartoon of St. Anne with the Virgin and Child and made a copy of it (Plate 8). At that time the pen was still Michelangelo's only drawing implement, but his technique has become looser and no longer shows those regular hatching lines reminiscent of the 'broad manner' of Florentine engravings.

1504 is another turning-point, not only in Michelangelo's art, but in the history of Florentine art as a whole. (It must not be forgotten that we are here speaking of a period during which the Medici were exiled from Florence, and that they had as little to do with the great artistic event of 1504 as they had with the achievements of Florentine painting from Giotto to Masaccio.) Two walls facing each other in the great Council Hall at the Palazzo Vecchio were to be adorned with paintings, and the Gonfaloniere of the city entrusted the task to the two best artists. The paintings were never executed, but the cartoons alone were outstanding enough to usher in a new epoch in Italian painting, again under Florentine hegemony. Leonardo chose the theme of the cavalry battle at Anghiari, while Michelangelo depicted an attack on bathing soldiers during the campaign against Pisa.

Michelangelo's cartoon was executed in chalk, charcoal and white lead. He represented nude human beings in every possible attitude, turning and perspective foreshortening. This cartoon was the foundation of his fame as a painter. His knowledge of the human body—a knowledge based on anatomical studies and on observation of nature and Hellenistic sculptures—had already been proclaimed on two occasions—in the Dead Christ of the Pietà for St. Peter's and in the gigantic figure of David which then stood before the entrance to the Palazzo Vecchio. The fidelity to nature shown in these two figures by far surpasses anything produced in the Quattrocento, even the works of Verrocchio, Leonardo, Mantegna and Signorelli; in them, and in the battle cartoon, a direct link was forged with antique art in the representation of the nude, thus fulfilling one of the aspirations of the Renaissance. Scores of artists made drawings after this cartoon, among them Granacci, Raphael, Daniele da Volterra, Berruguete, Perino del Vaga, Rosso, Pontormo, Andrea del Sarto and the brothers Zuccaro. The cartoon was cut up during Michelangelo's lifetime. Cellini brought a fragment of it back from France to Florence; other portions of it were preserved in Mantua and Turin until the early years of the seventeenth century. All that we possess of it to-day, if we exclude copies, are a few preliminary studies by Michelangelo's hand (e.g. Plates 17–19).

These studies for the cartoon were a preparation for the figures on the ceiling of the Sistine Chapel, and their technique is that of the Sistine drawings. For the cartoon Michelangelo chose soft drawing materials, charcoal and chalk, with which he appears to have achieved effortlessly the effects of a painter. He used the same materials for most of the Sistine drawings and also, for the first time, red chalk (Plates 27–30). When he still uses the pen, he no longer does so in the old way reminiscent of an engraving, but loosely and easily, just like the ductus of a pen in writing, sometimes in a cursory and sometimes in a calligraphic manner (Plates 25, 26). On a drawing in London, and on another at Oxford (Plates 25 and 32) we see the two techniques side by side. In the sketches of the following years—e.g. in those made for Sebastiano del Piombo (Plates 39–41 and 43)—he continues to use the soft technique of black and red chalk, with only unimportant developments.

As for the figures on the ceiling of the Sistine Chapel, especially the nude youths, they would have been inconceivable without the preparation afforded by the battle cartoon. To give an example, the drawing of the Ignudo sitting with his arm propped up behind him (Plate 26) is a repetition of a figure in the cartoon. There is only one novel element in the Sistine figures—the significance of their body movements.

In Greek art of the best period movements invariably had a purpose—a youth putting on the victor's wreath, extracting a thorn from his foot or throwing a discus, or a faun playing the castanets. In late Greek art expressive movements make their appearance—the reaction of a body to some external event. Fear and the expression of fear are fundamentally the same in antique Niobid reliefs and in Michelangelo's battle cartoon, and the mother of the Niobids—to keep to one example—expresses her grief with the same gestures as the Mother of God in Michelangelo's Pietà. So long as an external cause is perceptible and the gesture is a comprehensible reaction to a single influence, it is an expressive movement.

In the youths, Prophets and Sibyls on the ceiling of the Sistine Chapel, however, the movements become a language of the soul—they are emotional movements, having no purpose and provoked by no external cause; like the gestures of a dancer they symbolize the inner life; they are provoked, not by events, but by states of mind, they are a silent dialogue between the human soul and its destiny, between the soul and eternity; they have no beginning and no end, and are as hard to understand and susceptible of as many interpretations as cries rising from the depths.

The emotional movement is the chief motive of Michelangelo's art; he was the first to render it, and down to his last works he continued to develop it, renouncing it only in the very last of all. Michelangelo expressed the awakening to life in his 'Adam' and his 'Aurora'; absorption in dreams and darkness in his 'Dying Captive' and his 'Night'; the sinking into the abyss of one's own thoughts in his 'Jeremiah' and his 'Pensieroso'. The Captives, writhing in their fetters (Plates 24, 32), are struggling to achieve a freedom which is granted only after the dissolution of all earthly bonds. On the ceiling of the Sistine Chapel and afterwards Michelangelo expressed all the tendencies of the soul through the contortions of the human body.

From first to last Michelangelo had no feeling for landscape, for the world of plants, for the portrait as reproduction of the features of an individual human being, no feeling for the beauty of earth and sky or for all the phenomena of colour and light. In this he is quite distinct from his contemporaries Leonardo, Titian and Giorgione, and also from Grünewald and Dürer. We know that Michelangelo made portraits of Pope Julius II and of Tommaso de' Cavalieri, but in them he probably paid as little attention to lifelikeness as he did in his statues of Lorenzo and Giuliano. When he draws large heads (Plates 27, 28, 65, 66, 103) we can detect the use of a model, but there is no attempt to penetrate the model's character. We possess no landscape drawing by his hand. When he cannot dispense with landscape in a painting, it is a primitive, stony landscape, such as might have emerged from the waters on the day the earth was created—bare and devoid of vegetation, wild and empty. Everything Michelangelo had to express, he expressed through human beings—through the symbol of the human form and the signs of bodily movements. Michelangelo fashioned a language for the expression of that which cannot be spoken.

The preliminary work in the form of drawings for the Sistine Chapel ceiling must have been enormous, yet of the thousands of drawings for the pictures and individual figures, of studies for heads, hands and other parts of the body, for draperies and gestures, and lastly of the hundreds of cartoons, practically all have been lost. The cartoons were burned by order of the master, when he gave up his house in Rome in 1518; only the cartoon for the 'Drunkenness of Noah' came into the possession of his friend Bindo Altoviti in Florence, and that, too, has long since disappeared.

The next turning-point in Michelangelo's graphic style occurred while he was working on his sculptures for the Medici chapel.[4] The change began with the presentation drawings

---

[4] The sketches for the Medici chapel are not affected by this stylistic break; in any case, they are not numerous, and many of them are of doubtful authenticity (e.g. Plates 59–60). A group of pen-drawings from this period (Plates 44–46, 53–58) would appear, at least on superficial examination, to belong to an earlier period; but I have given in the Catalogue my reasons for dating them 1520–25.

for Perini, and the new manner was so completely different that until recent times the authenticity of these drawings was not generally acknowledged.

The time between the forty-fifth and sixtieth years of his life was Michelangelo's erotic period. The chief artistic outcome of these tendencies, illusions and heart-searchings was the group of the 'Victor', created at the same time as the figures for the Medici chapel. The metaphor contained in the 'Victor' is, I believe, not difficult to interpret. We need only think of the self-portrait of Cristofano Allori as the head of Holofernes in the hand of the beautiful Judith, in order to be able to guess the meaning of Michelangelo's marble youth kneeling over a prostrate old man. It may be that Gherardo Perini posed as model for this 'Victor', and perhaps also for the profile head of a young man with ear-rings and head-ornaments, stylistically related to the presentation drawings (Plate 65). Michelangelo made the acquaintance of this young man in 1522 and exchanged letters with him. We have documentary proof that Michelangelo drew a portrait of Tommaso de' Cavalieri, whose acquaintance he made ten years after he met Perini, and we also learn from a letter that he portrayed in a drawing the boy Cecchino Bracci. Mini, another of Michelangelo's favourites, was apprenticed to him in 1523 at the age of seventeen. Though the master never bought for him pink hose and capes of silver brocade, as Leonardo had done for his young pupil Salai twenty-five years before, he seems to have been lavish in presenting him with drawings. The last of these youthful friends of Michelangelo's was Febo di Poggio, whom he met in Florence shortly before his departure for Rome, and who sent him a letter which is not far short of blackmail: 'When you left you told me that, if I needed anything, I was to apply to that friend of yours. Now I need money and Signor G[ti] is not here. I want to buy myself new clothes in order to go to the horse-races at Monte,[5] where Signor G[ti] is also. I went to the bank, but there they told me they had no instructions from you. . . . I must ask you to be so good as to provide a little for me . . . and don't fail to answer me.' To him, as to Cavalieri, Michelangelo wrote passionate poems. A number of other love-poems are of somewhat earlier date and, I believe, addressed to Gherardo Perini. Here is a translation by Iris Holland Rogers of one of these sonnets:

> O noble soul, what beauty we can see
> Reflected in those limbs so chaste and dear,
> In which the work of heaven and nature here
> Creates a paragon of harmony:
> O gracious soul, within must surely be
> Those qualities which in your face appear
> Of mercy, love and pity; virtues rare,
> Which yet with your rare beauty well agree.
> By beauty I am bound, by love enslaved,
> While pity's touch and mercy's gentle glance
> Have filled my heart with deepest hope of grace.
> What law or earthly government depraved,
> What cruelty now or soon, or evil chance,
> Forbids grim death to spare this lovely face?

It is not my task to investigate the nature, or the unnaturalness, of these relationships. I have been obliged to discuss the psychological circumstances to the extent I have done, in order to explain the significance of the drawings made at this time—especially the presentation drawings for Perini and Cavalieri.

---

[5] According to Frey, *Monte* means Monte San Savino, or some other place near Florence or Pisa. *Signor G[ti]* may mean Giannotti.

To this period belong the designs for the 'Samson and Delilah', 'Venus and Cupid', the 'Rape of a Woman' and the 'Leda', the erotic character of which does not need to be further stressed (Plates 17, 62, 66 and 67), but at the same time Michelangelo also made his designs for the 'Noli me tangere', the 'Risen Christ', 'Christ in Limbo', the 'Three Crosses' and the 'Deposition', as well as the sketches for the 'Last Judgement' (Plates 71, 75–81, 87–90, 98–104). This list shows the conflict between the erotic and the religious tendencies in his mind.

In 1545 Aretino wrote to Michelangelo, reproaching him for failing to keep his promise to send him drawings—'only the Gherardos and the Tommasos can expect favours from you'.

The three drawings Michelangelo gave to Gherardo Perini are still extant. One of them (Plates 47, 51), showing women's heads executed with a pronounced sense for ornamentation and calligraphy, is interesting only on account of the unusual technique. The second (Plate 49), depicting a Fury, a head with fluttering hair and gaping mouth, symbolizes the madness of love, and was probably inspired by some lines of Ariosto. The third (Plate 50), 'Venus, Mars and Cupid', expresses that terrible form of love which resorts to arms and destruction.

The presentation drawings for Tommaso de' Cavalieri and an unknown friend owe their origin to the same state of mind. In these drawings the artist's thoughts are passionately engaged with the problem of temptation, sin and atonement.

From the point of view of religious symbolism the drawings may be interpreted as follows:

The Archers: The invulnerability of the protected soul (Plate 73).

Tityus: The sin and punishment of illicit sexual indulgence, or the torments of a man who through sensuality has become godless (Plate 74).

Phaëthon: The penalty of arrogance, or the fall resulting from desire for that which is not permitted (Plates 94–96).

The Dream: The five sins of passion, or the terrible awakening of the sinner to consciousness of himself (Plate 93).

The Bacchanal of Children: The abasement of mankind through sin (Plate 92).

A sixth drawing (Plate 68), the *Labours of Hercules*—his struggles with the lion, the giant and the nine-headed hydra—coincides exactly with the three examples given in Landini's dialogues, in which Hercules is the representative of the *Vita Activa* and fights against evil in the course of his journeys, as the Apostles did after him.[6]

Some of these drawings were made in Florence, others in Rome. In the autumn of 1534 Michelangelo transferred his residence to Rome.

Florence, Venice, Ferrara and other Italian cities had their local schools of painting, differing clearly from one another and far less closely related than dialects of the same language. In this respect they may be compared with the schools of painting in the Germanic countries, where Cologne and Nuremberg, Colmar and Basle, the Tyrol and Vienna used completely different languages in their art. In Italy, Rome occupied a place of its own as an artistic centre. It was the only city which had witnessed a direct continuation of antiquity down to the days of the Renaissance. In the other cities the rebirth of the antique had a literary origin; in Rome, where ruins and statues were visible to the eyes of succeeding generations as tangible presences, the Renaissance was derived, not from books, but from stones. The Belvedere Apollo, the Laocoön and the river-gods

---

[6] The lost drawing of 'Ganymede' and the above-mentioned nine presentation drawings (of which three were for Perini, three for Cavalieri, and three for unknown friends) are more fully discussed in the Catalogue, where I have quoted Virgil, Dante, Savonarola, etc., in support of my interpretations.

had merely remained hidden in the earth until the descendants of those who once had owned and imitated them had proved themselves, by means of their own art, to be worthy of these treasures, and now they were restored, comprehensible and enthusiastically welcomed as the cream of a great inheritance, to the hands of these descendants. Rome was the city of the Popes, and the Popes were the heirs of the Cæsars. Rome, the seat of the Catholic Imperium, had the ability to assimilate artists from the most varied cities and schools, to fill them with the Roman spirit—in both the old and the new sense (just as in the Rome of the Cæsars there had been very little difference between Roman and Greek sculptors). When Michelangelo arrived in Rome for the first time, in 1496, there were in the city artists from many provinces who had just completed, or were still engaged upon, important works: there were to be seen new frescoes by Mantegna, Perugino, Pinturicchio, Filippino Lippi, and Antonio Pollaiuolo's monuments to the Popes—great works of Roman Renaissance art.

Michelangelo's removal to Rome in 1534 and his work on the 'Last Judgement' were the foundations of the Roman school of 'Mannerism'.

A new style heralds the dawn of a new period. The end of the heathen Renaissance had come and the Christian Renaissance now began, as a long prepared religious revival.

Religion, like art, poetry, philosophy, fashions and morals, has a stylistic history of its own. The Renaissance had three great antique textbooks—the Bible, Plato and Aristotle. Christianity once again became an antique religion. In Botticelli's pictures we cannot distinguish Venus from the Madonna; nor, in Raphael's, the Greek philosophers from the Fathers of the Church; nor, in Michelangelo's, Hercules from Christ nor David from Apollo. But in Rome people began to doubt the admissibility of this concordance. The spiritual laws of the Renaissance, the revival of heathen antiquity, were conceived, in Florence, by enthusiastic humanists; the Counter-Reformation was an act of State and originated in Rome.

When a sword lies buried for a long time in the earth the sharp blade is consumed by rust, but the golden hilt is perfectly preserved. It is thus only by means of a laborious reconstruction that we can form a picture of the religious struggles at that time; the art of the period, however, still stands clear and untarnished in all its splendour before our eyes.

The religious revival in Italy, the course of which began about 1540, did not form part of the Reformation; it was a Catholic movement. Here we have only to consider that section of it which concerned Michelangelo.

In 1541 Pope Paul III appointed Cardinal Pole, a distant cousin of King Henry VIII of England, to be governor of the Patrimonium Petri, the oldest part of the Papal States, with residence at Viterbo. Here Pole gathered around him those who shared his views, among them the priest Carnesecchi, who many years later was burned at the stake, and the religious poet Flaminio. The latter collaborated in the writing of a book which appeared at Venice in 1542, and was at once placed on the Index as heretical—Benedetto's 'Of the mercy of the Crucified Christ', a work to which Flaminio gave its final stylistic form, and the mere possession of which was punished by the Inquisition with death.

Cardinal Pole and his circle, the 'Spirituali', were associated with a number of men who were working for a purification of the Catholic Church, men such as the Venetian Gasparo Contarini, and the preacher Ochino. Of the latter, who at the time was preaching in Rome, only a few miles from Viterbo, Agostino Gonzaga wrote to Ferrara: 'Ochino lives like a saint. . . . His convincing persuasiveness is seconded by a most magnificent voice. All Rome flocks to his sermons . . . The Marchesa di Pescara never misses one of them. She is living in cloistral retirement with the sisters of San Silvestro and receives no visitors.'

head may have had some connexion with the Piccolomini altar. The contract concluded with Michelangelo in 1501 (and renewed in 1504) stipulates expressly that sketches shall be made. The arm and the face, looking downwards, have points of similarity to the 'St. James the Great', and the 'St. Peter' might also serve for purposes of comparison. (Valentiner and Tolnay call the St. James *Peter* and the St. Peter, *Paul;* KdK, p. 158; Tolnay, I, Figs. 188 and 194.)

The sketch of the nude youth belongs to the same period as the Battle Cartoon. Under the right knee there is a hint of a shadow (not a *pentimento*), so that the attitude may be presumed to be the same as that of the climbing man on the left of the Holkham copy, viz., with the knee on the edge of the bank and the left leg hanging down into the water. This would enable us to date the sketch about 1504, which also seems to me to agree with the style.

18. NUDE SEEN FROM THE BACK. Pen and ink; below, two sketches in black chalk. 10½ × 7¾ in. Florence, Casa Buonarroti (No. 9F).

Sketches for the Battle Cartoon (1504).

There is another version of this drawing in Oxford (BB. 1559 *verso*), showing a further elaboration of the same figure.[10] Berenson calls the Oxford drawing 'one of Michelangelo's best pen and ink sketches', but Tolnay describes it as a copy; Baumgart, too, rightly excludes it from the genuine drawings.

19. NUDE SEEN FROM BEHIND, TWO PUTTI, LEG STUDY. Black chalk and pen. 12⅜ × 11¼ in. London, British Museum (1859-6-25-564 *recto*).

According to Baumgart the standing nude man is a study for the Battle Cartoon (1504), but was not used. The two Putti, still revealing the influence of Leonardo,[11] are related to the Pitti tondo (about 1504). The leg study, according to Tolnay, was drawn later (about 1520-25). Popp (20, p. 161 f.) dates the whole sheet from this period. This late dating was rejected by Thode (49, p. 268, No. 51), who dates the four lines of poetry written in the same dark-grey ink as the leg study 'about 1504'.

The four lines of poetry beneath the drawing (Frey, XXII) run as follows:

'Sol' io ardendo all' ombra mi rimango,
Quand' el sol de suo razi el mondo spoglia,
Ogni altro per piaciere, e io per doglia,
Prostrato in terra, mi lamento e piangho.'

('Alone I remain burning in the shadows,
When the sun withdraws his rays from the earth,
Others go to their pleasures, but I, prostrate with grief
Upon the ground, must mourn and weep.')

It seems to me that this strophe must belong, not to the early period about 1504, but to the time of Michelangelo's friendship

with Perini, after 1522; the handwriting also is not that of the early period.

The sketch of the leg with the drop-shaped toes may be compared with No. 58, which dates from the period of the Medici chapel. For this reason I date the two Putti about 1503-04 and the other two sketches about 1522-25. No. 20 (see below) is on the back of the sheet.

20. SKETCH FOR THE BRUGES MADONNA; THREE NUDE MEN. Black chalk and pen. 12⅜ × 11¼ in. London, British Museum (1859-6-25-564 *verso*).

There are no documents enabling us to determine exactly when the Bruges Madonna was executed. If we accept the assumption of Brinckmann (7, p. 22) and Valentiner (*Studies of Italian Renaissance Sculpture*, p. 216 f.) that the work was carried out between 1504 and 1506, we may consider this sketch to have been a first idea and date it about 1504.[12]

Brinckmann has given the correct explanation of the three nude figures: On the right, a man with a sword in his left hand (corresponding approximately to the nude seen from behind in No. 19); in the centre, a man making a beckoning gesture (similar to the gesture in No. 16); on the left, a crouching man doing up the sandal on his left foot. Brinckmann deems the figure group to be a sketch for the Battle Cartoon (1504). Popp (20, pp. 161-162) dates the whole sheet about 1530.

Doubts have been cast on the authenticity both of the chalk drawing and of the pen and ink sketch; as regards the Madonna, by Frey; as regards the group of three figures, by Baumgart (16, p. 32 f.). Baumgart believes that some mannerist from the entourage of Pontormo or Rosso has here combined three separate figures from the Battle Cartoon.[13] This supposition is supported by the very unusual style, almost reminding us of El Greco;[14] against it, we have the fact that the nude seen from behind on the front of the sheet is similar, though it is drawn more cursorily and loosely.

In my opinion it is impossible to accept the authenticity of the chalk sketch on the front of the sheet (No. 19) and at the same time to reject the group on the back; the drawings on both front and back are by the same hand. These sketches may be classed with a group of manneristic drawings which Michelangelo executed between 1516 and 1532, beginning with the red chalk sketches for Sebastiano del Piombo's 'Lazarus' and 'Flagellation', and including the later drawing (No. 43) which Sebastiano used about 1537 for his Pietà now at Ubeda, the 'Brazen Serpent', especially the figures on the left and right in the lower group which have remained at the stage of sketches (No. 91), and the sketches for the 'Resurrection' (e.g. Nos. 78 and 81). I believe that all these drawings are authentic, although I am aware that most of them have been attributed to Sebastiano and some of them to an anonymous pupil. Consequently, I date the pen and ink sketch of the Madonna about 1504 and the group of three male figures (like the nude on the front of the sheet) about twenty years later.

---

[10] To the same draughtsman a number of other copies can be ascribed. The 'nude seen from the back' of No. 18 appears in a more complete copy on the *recto* of BB. 1559, showing two figures and a horse; here the man is holding the stirrup, helping the other man to mount the horse. By the same hand as this drawing are, I believe, e.g. BB. 1397C, the copy of a part of the Battle Cartoon; BB. 1399A *verso*, a rider seen from the back; BB. 1742 *verso*, a man throwing a lance; and some more copies either from the Battle Cartoon or related to it.

[11] Windsor Castle, No. 12562. Emil Möller (in *Belvedere*, Vienna, 1926, IX, p. 18) reverses the relationship and ascribes the 'heroic' style of the Leonardo drawing to the influence of Michelangelo (about 1503-06).

[12] I think that this dating is correct. If, however, we consider the drawing to be a 'sketch from memory', then it would have to be dated after 1506, as the sculpture was not delivered until that year.

[13] If we wish to uphold the attribution to Michelangelo, we may use for purposes of comparison a sketch of a three-figure group (No. 39) which Michelangelo made in 1516 for Sebastiano del Piombo's 'Raising of Lazarus'. Compare also a group of three men in the lower right corner of No. 91.

[14] Compare, for example, the 'St. Sebastian' in Palencia Cathedral (*El Greco*, Phaidon Press, 1st edition, Plate 16; 2nd edition, Plate 40), painted not very long after El Greco's stay in Rome and his friendship with Giulio Clovio.

21. EIGHT NUDE CHILDREN. Pen and ink on greenish prepared paper. 14¾ × 9 in. London, British Museum (1887–5–2–117 *verso*).

The drawing dates from the same period as that on the front of the sheet (No. 16), or not much later. Brinckmann related the figures to the Child Christ of the Bruges Madonna (about 1504) and the infant St. John of the Taddei tondo in London (about 1504–05). The relationship to the Bruges Madonna had already struck the collector who, about 1600, twice wrote 'chosse di Brugis' on the sheet.

The sheet also contains some sketches in lead-point which have almost disappeared, e.g. on the left, beneath the outline sketch of the little St. John, the profile of a woman, and on the right a repetition of the infant St. John.

No. 16 (see above) is on the front of the sheet.

22–23. BATTLE OF HORSEMEN; NUDE FIGURE; DRAPED FIGURE; SEVERAL LIGHT SKETCHES FOR FIGURES ON THE FRONT OF THE SHEET; SKETCHES FOR ORNAMENTS FOR THE BASE OF A PILLAR OF THE TOMB OF POPE JULIUS. Pen and ink. 7¼ × 7 in. London, British Museum (1895–9–15–496 *recto* and *verso*).

All the sketches on the front and back of this sheet date from the same time. The ornaments are sketches for a relief on the base of the pillar on the extreme left of the tomb of Pope Julius, as Frey (13B) already pointed out (cf. Laux, *Juliusmonument*, pp. 109 and 189). The contract was made in March, 1505, and the drawing must have been made soon afterwards, either in 1505, while Michelangelo was still in Rome, or, more probably, in the summer of 1506 in Florence.

On May 2, 1506, Michelangelo wrote to Giuliano da Sangallo offering to continue in Florence his work on the tomb of Julius; judging from a letter of Balducci's dated May 9, 1506 (Gotti, II, 52), about this time he seems to have resumed work on the Battle Cartoon (Thode, I, 349); simultaneously, i.e. during the summer of 1506, he was also working on the 'St. Matthew' for Florence Cathedral (Valentiner, *Studies of Italian Renaissance Sculpture*, p. 219; Baumgart, 16, p. 17).

In April, 1505, Michelangelo had received the last payment from the Opera del Duomo for four figures of Apostles (Frey, Vol. II, p. 9; Valentiner, *op. cit.*, p. 219). Thode has already pointed out that the two sketches for an Apostle on the front of this sheet should not be identified as sketches for the St. Matthew, as they frequently are; we must assume that they were for another figure of an Apostle, which Michelangelo never began in sculpture.[15]

Lastly, I believe that the sketch of a battle of horsemen, which has always been held to be a first design for a part of the cartoon of the Battle of Cascina, is really a free copy of Leonardo's Battle of Anghiari. In Florence during the same year, 1506, Raphael copied another portion of Leonardo's cartoon,[16] and a few years earlier Michelangelo himself had copied in the same free manner Leonardo's cartoon for the 'St. Anne' (No. 8).

Berenson is the only critic who has disputed the authenticity of the sketches of ornaments.

The sheet has been cut on the left.

From the Lempereur, Dyce and Malcolm collections.

A drawing in the Uffizi showing the same figure of an Apostle, similar ornaments, the figure seen from the back in No. 19, etc., which Frey (233F), Brinckmann (Plate 8) and Valentiner (*Studies of Italian Renaissance Sculpture*, 1950, Fig. 224) reproduce as authentic, is recognized as an imitation by Berenson (1625 and 1645A), Thode (No. 215) and Baumgart (16, p. 31); Tolnay (17, p. 185) rightly describes this drawing as an old forgery.

There seems to be a lingering echo of the Apostle on No. 22 in Raphael's pen and ink sketch for the Dante in his 'Parnassus' (Fischel, V, 247).

24. SKETCH OF A CAPTIVE, PUTTO, WINGED HEAD OF AN ANGEL, ETC. Pen and ink. 15¾ × 8¼ in. Paris, Louvre (Inv. No. 688 *verso*). On the back of No. 10.

The Mercury-Apollo here appears traced in black chalk, but in the original attitude, with one arm hanging down free, not laid across the breast; the attributes, the winged hat and the viola, are also omitted. According to Berenson, this tracing is not by Michelangelo, nor can the profile head, in the exact middle of the sheet, be by him, since its technique is identical with that of the Madonna drawing in Berlin (BB. 1396; by the Master of the Manchester Madonna; see Excursus II, p. 180, and Fig. 1a–b). Frey rejected the attribution to Michelangelo

Details from drawings by the Master of the Manchester Madonna

FIG. 1a.—From a drawing in Berlin (see Plate No 176).
FIG. 1b.—From a drawing in Paris (see Plate No. 24).

of the head of a man with a feather in his hat and of the winged angel's head; the leg study and the little nude lying obliquely below on the right are likewise by the hand of the same assistant. On this side of the sheet there thus remain only two authentic sketches—the putto and the Captive.

The putto, a sketch by Michelangelo's own hand, was used by the Master of the Manchester Madonna—to whom, in my opinion, altogether six of the sketches on this sheet ought to be attributed—for the infant St. John in his large picture of the Madonna (London, National Gallery, No. 809; see Popp, 55, p. 6 f.).

The Captive sketch, which has some connexion with the contract for the tomb of Pope Julius signed in 1505, enables us

---

[15] The cancellation of the contract for the twelve Apostles on December 18, 1505, did not deter Michelangelo from carrying on with the work during the summer of 1506. Valentiner believes the sketch of an Apostle to be a preliminary drawing for a St. Thomas for the Piccolomini altar, in connexion with a contract concluded in October, 1504. As Michelangelo did not send the Mouscron Madonna, which according to Valentiner was also originally intended for the Piccolomini altar, to Bruges until August, 1506, he might have begun work on the substitute about this time. I am here discussing merely the date, not Valentiner's hypotheses.

[16] Fischel, *Raphael*, 1948, Plate 53 (F. IV, 210). This composition appears in a similar form, but partially inverted, in the left half of the 'Victory of Constantine' (Gronau, *Raphael*, 1923, KdK 204).

to date the sheet. Here again we must remember the letter which Michelangelo wrote from Florence on May 2, 1506, to Giuliano da Sangallo, asking him to obtain the Pope's consent to Michelangelo's continuing his work on the tomb of Julius in Florence instead of in Rome.

The lines of poetry near the Captive, a strophe of Petrarch's, are in Michelangelo's handwriting, here having the same character as in No. 23, which I have also dated 1506.

25. SKETCH FOR A COMPARTMENT IN THE CEILING OF THE SISTINE CHAPEL; HAND AND ARM STUDIES. Pen and black chalk. $10\frac{5}{8} \times 15\frac{1}{8}$ in. London, British Museum (1859-6-25-567 recto).

This pen drawing in bistre is connected with Michelangelo's original plan for the frescoes in the Sistine Chapel, viz., that the twelve Apostles were to be painted in the spandrels and the remaining surfaces filled with ornaments.[17] On May 10, 1508, Michelangelo received the first payment, and this is approximately the date of the sketch. The Apostle may possibly have been drawn from a lay figure.[18]

The arm and hand studies are probably of later date, about 1509. The study for the left hand was used three times, for the Adam, the Amon and the Jesse.[19] The studies for the right hand and right arm were used twice, for an Ignudo and for a figure in the Ezechias lunette.[20]

On the back are a pen and ink drawing of a seated figure (not by Michelangelo) and a drapery study in black chalk, perhaps originally by Michelangelo's hand, but since much over-drawn. The drapery may have been used (inverted) for the Jesse lunette.

Formerly in the Casa Buonarroti.

26. STUDIES FOR IGNUDI OF THE SISTINE CHAPEL CEILING. Black chalk, brown and black ink. $7\frac{1}{2} \times 9\frac{5}{8}$ in. London, British Museum (1859-6-25-568 recto).

Only the sketch on the left in brownish ink over a preliminary drawing in black chalk is certainly by Michelangelo. In the preliminary sketch the figure was kneeling on its right knee with the left leg up; the over-drawing in ink first of all partly followed the lines of the chalk and Michelangelo then altered the pose into one of kneeling on both knees.[21] The figure was probably, as most critics say, conceived as a promemoria for an Ignudo.

The other Ignudo sketches, which are in a blacker ink, seem doubtful, and Tolnay has attributed them to an anonymous assistant.

On the back of the sheet is a study of the nude in soft black chalk (No. 38).

Formerly in the Casa Buonarroti.

27. HEAD STUDY. Black chalk (heightened with white by another hand). $12 \times 8\frac{1}{2}$ in. Paris, Louvre (Inv. No. 860 verso).

Study for the Ignudo on the left above the Isaiah on the Sistine

Chapel ceiling. In the fresco the head has a fillet fixed round it, and there are also other minor modifications of the sketch. The treatment of the hair and the spotty forms of the shadows remind us of No. 29; the long, oblique lines of the hatching are found again in No. 28. Retouching by another hand, consisting especially in the addition of reflected lights in white chalk, have impaired the quality of the drawing. None the less, like Thode and Berenson, I believe that this drawing is authentic.

On the other side of the sheet: the same Ignudo, in full length; black chalk, badly rubbed and consequently difficult to judge; probably not by Michelangelo.

28. STUDY OF A HEAD IN PROFILE; TWO SKETCHES OF A LEFT KNEE. Black chalk. $17\frac{1}{8} \times 11$ in. Florence, Uffizi (18718F).

The dating of this drawing is dependent on whether we wish to connect it with the Moses or with the Zechariah on the Sistine Chapel ceiling; if we date it about 1513, then it must have been intended for the Moses; if about 1509, then for the Zechariah. The profile of the Moses resembles the drawing far more than does the head of Zechariah; in the execution in fresco the receding forehead and the different form of the nose are at once noticeable. Since Pope Julius II—as all his portrait medals that can be dated prove—wore no beard until 1511, the drawing cannot be a portrait of him unless we date it after that year. K. A. Laux (Michelangelos Juliusmonument, Berlin, 1943, p. 342) dates the drawing about 1513, and insists that it represents Julius II. This is at least correct in so far as the drawing, if intended for the Moses, must relate to the 1513 contract for the tomb, not to the original contract of 1505. I myself—though I cannot altogether dispel my own doubts—would date it, from the style, about 1509.

On the back of the sheet are some silverpoint sketches which are not by Michelangelo.

A part of the blank paper margins is not included in our reproduction.

29. HEAD STUDY. Red chalk. $8\frac{5}{8} \times 6\frac{3}{4}$ in. Florence, Casa Buonarroti (No. 1).

Tolnay was the first to describe this drawing correctly, namely, as an inverted study for the head of the Prophet Jonah. In view of the technique, the previous theory of a relationship to the Doni Madonna (c. 1505) cannot be maintained,[22] and one characteristic feature of the head—the open mouth showing the teeth—is not found in that work. Stylistically the drawing is on a par with No. 30 and can be dated about 1511-12.

30. STUDIES FOR THE LIBYAN SIBYL. Red chalk. $11\frac{3}{8} \times 8\frac{1}{2}$ in. New York, Metropolitan Museum.

A copy of this drawing in the Uffizi does not include the large head below on the left, which is, moreover, a copy made by the hand of a pupil. The sketch of the upper part of the body and the hand beneath it are likewise copies.

Michelangelo's are the foot, the studies for toes and the nude figure, drawn from a male model, although intended for a female figure on the Sistine Chapel ceiling.

[17] Heinrich Wölfflin in Jahrbuch der preussischen Kunstsammlungen, XII, 1892, p. 178 f.

[18] Cf. Filarete, Book XXIV (ed. Oettingen, p. 654).

[19] L. Goldscheider, Michelangelo's Paintings, 2nd edition, London, 1948, Plates 15, 103, 113.

[20] Ibid., Plates 35, 111.

[21] This is also Thode's opinion. Berenson, and after him Tolnay, maintain that the kneeling on both knees was the original pose, but the preliminary chalk drawing contradicts this assumption.

[22] Bertini (15, p. 58) insists that this head was drawn for the Doni Madonna.

On the back of the sheet are sketches in black chalk by the same pupil who drew the large head, etc., on the front.

From the collection of Don Aurelio de Beruete in Madrid.

31. FEMALE SERVANT FOR THE JUDITH WITH THE HEAD OF HOLOFERNES. Pen and ink. 12¾ × 10¼ in. Paris, Louvre (Inv. 685 *verso*).

In its technique (with the strokes in a much more fluent manner and less even than in other drawings made about 1505) this drawing is akin to the other drawing on the front of the sheet (No. 35), to No. 36, the date of which is certain, and to Nos. 33 and 34. The two latter drawings I assign to the year 1513, during which the second project for the tomb of Pope Julius was made. The candelabrum, shaped like a vase, in the drawing we are considering also seems to me to be connected with this second design; in any case similar candelabra were projected to crown the tomb of Julius.

From October, 1511, until the death of the Pope (February 21, 1513) Michelangelo busied himself with the preparations for resumption of work on the tomb, while he was completing the spandrel pictures on the Sistine Chapel ceiling.[23] In January, 1512, Michelangelo's brother, Buonarroto di Simone, came to see him in Rome, probably in connexion with his project of acquiring a partnership in the banking house of Donato di Bertini in Florence. Officially, the partnership agreement was not concluded until 1513, but it may well be that the collaboration between Donato and Michelangelo's brother began earlier. These dates are important, because the drawing we are discussing is on a page from a ledger of the firm of Donato and Buonarroto, which gave Frey good reason for dating it about 1513. Later authors have tried to give it an earlier date (Thode, 1503-04; Baumgart, 1501-02; Tolnay, 1505). Berenson assumes that it was made 'after 1511'.

At the top on the left, underneath the seven lines of entries made by the bank clerk, we see, drawn upside-down, the head and upper part of an eagle. There are similar eagles on the base of a pulpit in Pisa Cathedral, between the statues of Prudence and Fortitude (A. Venturi, *Giovanni Pisano*, 1927, Plate 102), and on the Palazzo Comunale at Bologna; the latter was at one time wrongly attributed to Michelangelo. There is an antique prototype of this eagle, namely, that belonging to the Ganymede statue in Naples (No. 186, from the Farnese collection; reprod. W. Klein, *Praxiteles*, p. 129). Close to the eagle in the drawing there is one word in Michelangelo's handwriting, which is difficult to decipher, but may be 'androne'.

The title of the drawing is far from being certain. It has also been called 'Salome with the head of St. John the Baptist'. Baumgart (16, p. 46 f.) thinks that only the front of this sheet is authentic (No. 35), and attributes the back (No. 31) to the Master of the Manchester Madonna.

From the Mariette collection.

32. SKETCHES FOR THE SISTINE CHAPEL CEILING AND THE TOMB OF JULIUS. Red chalk and pen. 11⅜ × 7⅞ in. Oxford, Ashmolean Museum (No. 23).

Sketches in red chalk for the boy holding a roll of paper, in the fresco on the left behind the Libyan Sibyl, and right hand

of the Sibyl. At the top on the left, drawn with the pen, part of a cornice, presumably for the tomb of Julius, and six pen and ink sketches of bound Captives for the tomb.[24]

The red chalk drawings were made about 1511. The pen and ink sketches, which are invariably dated 1513, may have been a little earlier, since Michelangelo began to busy himself again with the tomb of Julius, at the latest in October, 1511, although the second contract was not concluded until after the death of the Pope on May 6, 1513. (This means that the *whole* drawing may possibly date from 1512.)

On the back of the sheet are leg studies in pen and ink.

From the Mariette, Lagoy and Lawrence collections.

33. SKETCHES FOR ONE OF THE SEATED FIGURES IN THE UPPER STORY OF THE TOMB OF JULIUS, AND A CARYATID PUTTO. Pen and ink. 16½ × 11 in. London, British Museum (1887-5-2-115 *recto*).

On May 6, 1513, Michelangelo signed a new contract with the heirs of the Pope for the tomb of Julius. In this contract we read *inter alia:* 'Round the sarcophagus six blocks will be arranged on which there will be six figures of equal size, all six in a sitting posture.'[25] Two of these figures represented Moses and Paul, two others Rachel and Leah; as regards the third pair, we do not know what they represented—probably

---

[24] Leonardo da Vinci uses similar figures of bound captives in his sketches for the Trivulzio monument (*Leonardo*, Phaidon edition, Plates 137 and 146). These designs of Leonardo's can be dated about 1511. As far as the technique is concerned, Michelangelo's sketches of Captives recall early pen and ink drawings by Leonardo, e.g. the St. Sebastian at Hamburg (see illustration, p. 179).

[25] W. Maurenbrecher (30, p. 296), Plate 2.

FIG. 2.—After Michelangelo: Detail from a design for the 1513 project for the tomb of Julius, in the Uffizi at Florence (BB. 1632).

---

[23] As Berenson has pointed out, this drawing may also be assumed to have had some connexion with the spandrel fresco of 'Judith and Holofernes' (1511-12).

St. Peter and another male figure. Michelangelo's original design, dating from 1513, is now preserved in the Berlin Print Room.[26] In the same collection there is a faithful copy of this original design by Michelangelo's pupil Jacomo Rocchetti (reproduced here opposite p. 13), in which we can recognize the two seated female figures on the left, and also the caryatid putti. It is possible that the sketch we are discussing was intended for the Leah—the figure farther back in the Rocchetti copy, the more difficult of the two to identify.

The same sitting figure, better recognizable than in the Rocchetti copy, also appears in a drawing at the Uffizi (see Fig. 2).

The lines drawn with the pen to the right of the female figure seem to show the tabernacle niche in profile.[27] The rest of the architecture which can be seen is a translucence from the back of the sheet, on which a pupil has drawn a religious scene with figures in antique costumes.

This drawing has hitherto been included among the designs for figures on the Sistine Chapel ceiling, because the draperies reminded the critics of the Persian Sibyl, and the position of the arms, of the Isaiah. That the technique of the drawing is quite different from that of others known to be designs for the Sistine Ceiling (e.g. Nos. 25, 26, 29, 30 and 32) has been

---

[26] BB. 1623. In a very bad state of preservation. I have an old photograph of this drawing on which one can see more than on the original, which in the meantime has almost completely disintegrated.

[27] Laux, *Juliusmonument*, p. 197. Cf. also Panofsky, *Studies in Iconology*, p. 188, and Figs. 131, 132, 136, 137.

FIG. 3.—After Michelangelo: Detail from a design for the 1513 project for the tomb of Julius, in the Berlin Print Room (BB. 1623).

ignored. As regards the soft pen technique, cf. No. 36, the date of which is certain.

From the Ottley and Lawrence collections.

34. SIBYL AND PUTTO, SKETCH FOR SECOND PROJECT FOR THE TOMB OF JULIUS. Pen and ink. 12¼ × 8⅝ in. Paris, Louvre (Inv. No. R.F. 4112 *verso*).

In the 1513 design for the tomb of Julius we see the seated putto on the right near the recumbent Pope, with the standing Sibyl further to the right (see Fig. opposite p. 13 and the detail reproduced on this page; cf. No. 33). This figure, which in its final execution was to have been far more than life-size, as shown in the drawing agrees almost exactly with a figure in Rocchetti's copy of the whole project: the head is bent forward, the right hand grasps a portion of the robe, the left arm is laid across the breast and the position of the feet is the same. The line and the hatching behind the figure serve to indicate the pilaster.

Various dates have been assigned to the drawing, the only correct one being that given by Berenson.[28]

The lines of poetry are written in three kinds of ink, one of which is the same as that used for the drawing. Thode (49, p. 268) dates them too early (1505-10), Frey (48, p. 236) too late (about 1524). The character of the handwriting seems to me to point also to the period around 1513. The upper part of the body of a putto on the lower edge of the drawing is a copy by a pupil (but not by Mini).

No. 48 is on the other side of the sheet.

From the Bernardo Buontalenti, Casa Buonarroti, Wicar, Earl Fitzwilliam and Léon Bonnat collections.

35. ST. ANNE WITH THE VIRGIN AND CHILD. Pen and ink on black chalk. 12¾ × 10¼ in. Paris, Louvre (Inv. No. 685 *recto*).

No. 31 is on the back of the sheet, and what has here already been said about it is, in general, also applicable to No. 35.

Stylistically, the drawing belongs to the same group as Nos. 33, 34 and 36, for which reason I agree with Frey and Demonts in dating it about 1513.[29] The ductus of the pen in the nude figure (below, across the sheet) is similar to that of the sketches of Captives on No. 32 and of the upper part of the figure, given only in outline, on No. 36.

As Johannes Wilde (46, p. 60 f.) has pointed out, the Virgin in this drawing is a free copy of Giovanni Pisano's Sibyl on the pulpit in Pistoia.

The sketch of the nude man can be brought into hypothetical relationship with the second contract for the Apostles for the cathedral in Florence. In his life of Andrea Ferrucci, Vasari says that the supervisors of the Opera del Duomo made contracts for five figures of Apostles with five masters—Benedetto [Rovezzano], Jacopo Sansovino, Baccio Bandinelli, Andrea Ferrucci and Michelangelo. The dates of the contracts with Andrea Ferrucci and Benedetto Rovezzano are known—

---

[28] *Drawings of Florentine Painters*, 1938, *Catalogue*, p. 212: 'These sketches are of no earlier date than 1510—and, I should think, not later than 1514.'

[29] Popp (45, Vol. LIX, p. 135) thinks that the figure of St. Anne was added later—about 1524. But the drawing, as Berenson has pointed out, reminds us of the Usina Group between Ezekiel and the Erythraean Sibyl. This portion of the Sistine frescoes was completed in September, 1512.

September and October, 1512[30]—and the statues were to be a St. Andrew and a St. John the Evangelist. Sansovino's contract, which was never executed, must have been concluded about 1513 during his stay in Florence. The contract for the figure of St. Peter, eventually executed by Baccio Bandinelli, is dated May 25, 1514, and January 25, 1515. In August, 1514, Michelangelo was again in Florence. He certainly did not feel indifferent when he heard that Bandinelli and other artists had been entrusted with the execution of the Apostle statues originally commissioned from him (contract of April 24, 1503). The sketch of a nude man was perhaps drawn for a St. Peter in competition with Bandinelli.

36. SKETCH FOR THE RISEN CHRIST MADE FOR METELLO VARI. Pen and ink on red chalk. $9\frac{3}{8} \times 8\frac{1}{4}$ in. London, Brinsley Ford collection.

The statue was commissioned on June 14, 1514, and this sketch of a torso was probably made about that time. The first version of the Christ, since lost, was at one time in the possession of Metello Vari. The second version was completed in 1521 and is now in Santa Maria sopra Minerva in Rome.
The sketches on the back of the sheet are—according to A. E. Popp—by the hand of Silvio Falcone (cf. B.B. 1702).
Formerly in the Lempereur, Heseltine and Henry Oppenheimer collections.

37. SKETCH FOR A CHRIST ON THE CROSS. Black chalk and bistre wash. $6\frac{1}{2} \times 4\frac{1}{8}$ in. Oxford, Library of Christ Church (No. C.13).

Dates from about 1515—later than the sketches of Captives on No. 32, and somewhat earlier than the drawing for Sebastiano del Piombo (No. 39).[31] At the top are two lines in Michelangelo's handwriting; at an angle, nine lines in the same handwriting, but crossed out; below, to the right of them, two lines in another hand; there is also writing on the back of the sheet.
Formerly in the collection of General John Guise (1765).

38. MALE TORSO. Black chalk. $9\frac{3}{4} \times 7\frac{1}{2}$ in. London, British Museum (1859-6-25-568 verso).

No. 26 is on the front of the sheet.
Berenson, who believes that this is a sketch for a dead Christ, dates it from the time of the Sistine ceiling frescoes, i.e. about 1510; Thode assigns it to the period of the 'Last Judgement', i.e. about 1534. I notice a stylistic relationship to the figure on the left in No. 39, and I ascribe the obvious differences to the fact that different drawing materials were used. In my opinion, the drawing should be dated about 1516.
A part of the blank paper margins is not included in the reproduction.

39. SKETCHES FOR SEBASTIANO DEL PIOMBO'S RAISING OF LAZARUS. Red chalk. $7\frac{5}{8} \times 12\frac{3}{4}$ in. Bayonne, Musée Bonnat (No. 682).

See under No. 40.
Müntz, Thode and Johannes Wilde attribute the drawing to Michelangelo.

(See Karl Frey, *Sammlung ausgewählter Briefe an Michel-agniolo Buonarroti*, Berlin, 1899; letter from Rome, dated January 19, 1516, from Leonardo Sellaio to Michelangelo).

40. STUDY FOR SEBASTIANO DEL PIOMBO'S RAISING OF LAZARUS. Red chalk. $10 \times 4\frac{3}{4}$ in. London, British Museum (1860-7-14-2).

Vasari, who knew both Michelangelo and Sebastiano del Piombo well and had personal contact with them, says in his life of Sebastiano that the *Raising of Lazarus* was 'painted by Sebastiano under the direction of Michelangelo and partly after drawings made by the latter'.[32] During the last fifty years, various critics from Franz Wickhoff[33] to Berenson[34] and Tolnay[35] have rejected the attribution to Michelangelo of this and a number of other drawings, and have assigned them to Sebastiano. Sebastiano's latest biographer, Pallucchini,[36] also accepts their views. Charles Loeser condemned No. 40 as an imitation.
Michelangelo made several sketches for Sebastiano's 'Lazarus'. The first was one with three figures, now in Bayonne (No. 39), which Müntz was the first rightly to attribute to Michelangelo.[37] Two other drawings are here reproduced (Nos. 40 and 41). All these drawings date from 1516-17.
The clumsy studies of feet at the bottom of No. 40 are probably by Sebastiano.
Formerly in the collections of the Casa Buonarroti, Wicar, Lawrence, King William II of Holland, and Woodburn.

41. HEAD OF LAZARUS. Black chalk over red chalk, corrections in pen and ink. $12\frac{7}{8} \times 8\frac{1}{4}$ in. London, British Museum (1895-9-15-498 verso).

This drawing of a head was generally held to be an inverted sketch for the head of the Adam on the Sistine Chapel ceiling, while the hand was supposed to be a sketch for the hand of God the Father in the 'Creation of Adam'.[38] Berenson was the first to recognize that the head belonged to Sebastiano del Piombo's 'Raising of Lazarus', and in fact suggested that we have here probably a reworking by Michelangelo of a drawing by Sebastiano. The sheet clearly reveals three states: first, a weak preliminary drawing in red chalk; then a timid and a more vigorous over-drawing in black chalk; and lastly, amplifications with the pen. It is especially in these strokes of the pen that Berenson recognizes Michelangelo's work, whereas it is precisely in these pen and ink corrections that Tolnay professes to see the work of Sebastiano.
Like Berenson, I believe that Michelangelo reworked a weak red and black chalk drawing by Sebastiano with black chalk and the pen, to such an extent that hardly anything of Sebastiano's original sketch can now be seen. The sketch of a hand in the left bottom corner may be by Sebastiano, since it reminds us of the right hands in the portraits he painted about this time (cf. Pallucchini, Plates 36 and 46).

---

[30] *Vasari*, Milanesi edition, 1879, Vol. IV, pp. 478, 479 (Note 2) and 532.
[31] Thode (Vol. III, p. 680) dates it from 'the period of the work on the Medici tombs'; Berenson, on the other hand, 'scarcely later than 1515'.

[32] *Vasari*, Milanesi edition, 18, Vol. V, p. 570: '. . . . Sotto ordine e disegno in alcune parti di Michelagnolo.' The painting is now in the National Gallery, London.
[33] 1899, in *Jahrbuch der preussischen Kunstsammlungen*, XX, p. 204.
[34] 1903 and 1938, *The Drawings of the Florentine Painters*.
[35] 1948, *The Medici Chapel*, p. 20.
[36] 1944, *Sebastian Viniziano*, pp. 49-50, 124-126, 177.
[37] 1896, in *Gazette des Beaux-Arts*, I, p. 121.
[38] This would involve dating it about 1509, which is certainly much too early.

No. 14, dating from a much earlier period, is on the front of the sheet.[39]

42. TRITON. Charcoal drawing on a wall on the first floor of the Villa Michelangelo at Settignano. About $3\frac{1}{2} \times 5$ ft.

This almost lifesize charcoal drawing appears to be derived from Mantegna's two engravings of the 'Battle of Tritons' (B. 17–18; about 1490; Kristeller, p. 394). It was first discussed in detail and claimed for Michelangelo by C. H. Wilson (1876). Tolnay holds it to be the oldest work by Michelangelo that has been preserved, executed before he entered Ghirlandaio's workshop, that is to say, when the artist was twelve years old! Thode stressed the bad state of preservation of the 'fresco' and thought that it 'could not possibly be a youthful work'; he does not, however, venture any opinion as to whether it is authentic or not. Frey said of it: 'To-day a rough, much reworked drawing, the original form of which is barely recognizable; if it is really by Michelangelo, it must belong to a late period in his work.' Johannes Wilde (46, p. 46) and Baumgart (16, p. 11) refrain from expressing an opinion, on the ground that they have not seen the original. Berenson assigns it to the period between the Sistine Chapel ceiling and the 'Last Judgement', that is to say, between 1512 and 1534.

I have seen this drawing several times, and could detect Michelangelo's original and unadulterated work only in the back of the head and ear and in the draperies. Although for this reason I must accept Frey's doubts, I am nevertheless inclined to believe that the drawing is authentic. In its general lines it agrees fairly well with the chalk drawing at Bayonne (No. 39), and I therefore consider it not improbable that it was executed about 1516.[40]

---

[39] The question as to how Sebastiano came to be in possession of a drawing by Michelangelo and to begin a sketch on the back of it, can be answered in two ways: firstly, we learn from Vasari that Michelangelo gave Sebastiano a number of drawings, and, secondly, in July and at the beginning of December, 1516, Michelangelo spent a few weeks in Rome.

[40] In that year Michelangelo was frequently in Florence. His house in the Via Mozza was not finished until the summer of 1519.

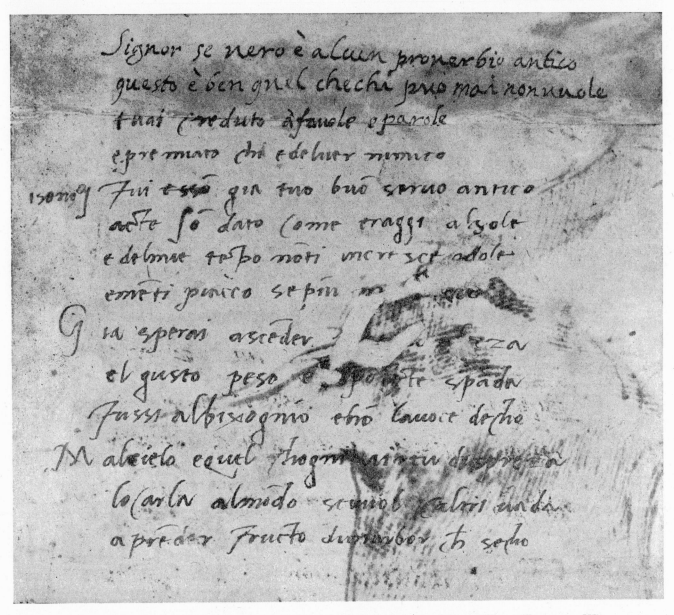

FIG. 4.—A sonnet in Michelangelo's handwriting; detail from the *verso* of drawing No. 44 (Frey, poem III).

43. STUDY FOR A PIETÀ. Black chalk. 10 × 12½ in. Paris, Louvre (Inv. No. 709).

This drawing is attributed by many critics to Sebastiano del Piombo, by others to Michelangelo.

Two facts must be taken into consideration. Firstly, E. Panofsky[41] has shown that Sebastiano used this drawing for his Pietà in Ubeda (Andalusia); secondly, as Johannes Wilde[42] observed, it is derived from an antique relief belonging to the heirs of Lorenzo Ghiberti (see Plates 143-146).

Even Berenson, who is normally anything but niggardly in attributing works to Sebastiano, assigns this drawing to Michelangelo on account of its outstanding quality, and this despite the fact that its connexion with the Ubeda Pietà is clear to him. The drawing has been given widely varying dates: Brinckmann dates it about 1508; Frey, about 1513; Berenson, about 1520; Wilde, about 1525; Thode, about 1530.

In my opinion it was made about 1519, immediately after Michelangelo moved to Florence. In style it still resembles the 'Lazarus' drawings of 1516, but in its feeling for form it is more akin to the Boboli Captives on which Michelangelo was particularly engaged in 1519.[43]

See also the note to No. 61.

Formerly in the collections of the Casa Buonarroti, Wicar, Lawrence and King William II of Holland.

44-45. THREE STUDIES OF HORSES AND A BATTLE SCENE. Pen and ink. 16¼ × 10 in. Oxford, Ashmolean Museum (No. 18).

Most critics have related these sketches to the Battle Cartoon and dated them about 1504-06. Miss A. E. Popp (20, p. 159) attempted to establish a relationship between this drawing and a projected lunette fresco in the Medici chapel, and suggested dating it about 1525; Tolnay agrees with her on this point.

In 1520, after the death of Raphael, a commission for frescoes in the Sala di Costantino in the Vatican was to be assigned. On April 12 Sebastiano del Piombo wrote to Michelangelo asking for his support against the assistants of Raphael.[44] Michelangelo tried to have the commission given to Sebastiano by writing to Cardinal Bibbiena, but it was finally assigned to Raphael's workshop. On July 3, 1520, Sebastiano wrote to Michelangelo concerning the projected frescoes in the Sala di Costantino: 'I believe that they want to have painted there a lot of battle pictures, and that is not a job for young men.' He goes on to say: 'To tell the truth, that is not a job for beginners, it is more suited to you. . . . If you are willing to undertake the work, there is much money and honour to be gained.'

Did Michelangelo, who for many years had been jealous of Leonardo and Raphael, take Sebastiano's suggestion seriously and draw these sketches at that time?

In any case, I find it impossible to assign an early date to this drawing (or to No. 46), and on this point am in agreement with Popp and Tolnay. Nevertheless, it seems to me that to

date it about 1520 accords better with the development of Michelangelo's draughtsmanship than dating it from the late period of the work on the Medici Chapel.

On the back of the sheet are a sonnet (Fig. 4) and four love-poems (Frey 48, poems II-VI), which likewise do not seem to fit in with an early dating.[45]

The sheet has been folded in the middle, so that four sides were available. The two inner sides are covered with the verses, while the two outer sides have been used for the upper and lower drawings, which are here reproduced facing each other in their original size.

From the Ottley and Lawrence collections.

46. COMBAT OF CAVALRY AND FOOT SOLDIERS. Pen and ink. 7⅜ × 10 in. Oxford, Ashmolean Museum (No. 16).

I date this drawing, too, about 1520—cf. the text to No. 45. Baumgart suggested that the drawing was made with the help of a manikin. A comparison with woodcuts in Erhard Schön's Unterweisung der Proportion und Stellung der Possen (i.e. of manikins), Nuremberg, 1538 and 1540, supports this assumption (cf. the battle scenes, D. IV and E. I, and the rearing horse, F. III).

From the Ottley and Lawrence collections.

47. THREE FEMALE PROFILES. Black chalk. 13⅜ × 9 in. Florence, Uffizi (No. 599E verso).

On the back of No. 51; presentation drawing for Gherardo Perini. Three letters from Perini to Michelangelo and the latter's reply have been preserved; all four letters are dated 1522. Berenson attributes this and all similar drawings to 'Andrea', an alleged workshop assistant of Michelangelo's; Morelli, on the other hand, was convinced that all these drawings were by Bacchiacca. Thode thought that No. 47 (and the drawing on the front of it, No. 51) were 'copies after drawings by the Master'.

In his life of Michelangelo, Vasari wrote: 'To his close friend, the Florentine nobleman Gherardo Perini, Michelangelo gave three folios with several heads in black chalk (a suo amicissimo . . . in tre carte alcune teste di matita nera . . .). After his death they came into the hands of the illustrious Signor Francesco de' Medici.' Aretino, in his venomous open letter of 1545, refers to these drawings: 'You should have kept your promise [to send a drawing] and with the greatest punctiliousness, in order thus to refute the calumny which asserts that no one can obtain favours from you, unless he be a Gherardo [Perini] or a Tommaso [Cavalieri]'.

The three drawings for Perini were first identified by Johannes Wilde (in the catalogue of the drawings at Windsor Castle, p. 264). They are my numbers 51 (with 47, on the back), 49 and 50.

48. TWO MADONNA STUDIES. Pen and ink. 12¼ × 8⅝ in. Paris, Louvre (Inv. No. R.F. 4112 recto).

No. 34 is on the back of the sheet.

Frey (48, p. 325) at first dated the drawing on the back about

---

[41] In Festschrift für Julius von Schlosser, Vienna, 1927, pp. 150-161. Cf. C. Justi, Miscellaneen (1908), II, p. 156: 'In S. Salvador at Ubeda there is still the large Pietà by Sebastiano del Piombo. . . . The motive is borrowed from the well-known Michelangelo drawing in the Louvre.'

[42] In Italian Drawings at Windsor Castle, London, 1949, p. 246. See also O. Fischel, Raphael, London, 1948, I, p. 192.

[43] Compare also the so-called 'bearded giant', Plates 70-72 in my edition of Michelangelo's Sculptures (Phaidon Press), 1950. The technical similarity to drawings No. 67 and 68 seems to speak against my dating and in favour of the date suggested by Thode, but these drawings reveal a more developed style which at the same time has become manneristic.

[44] All the documents relating to this are most easily accessible in Vincenzo Golzio, Raffaello nei Documenti, 1936, p. 125 f.

[45] Frey dates the sonnet about 1511 and assumes that it was addressed to Julius II; but he adds (p. 306): 'The sonnet, it is true, does not contain anything which definitely points to Julius II; one should rather think of Clement VII, whose "omo" Michelangelo called himself in 1518.' I believe that the sonnet can be connected with the quarrel Michelangelo had at the beginning of 1520 with Clement VII (at that time, Cardinal Giulio de' Medici) about some marble blocks reserved for Michelangelo's work on the façade of San Lorenzo, but carried off by the Opera del Duomo (Milanesi, Lett. 414; Thode, I, p. 377).

1513, and assigned the two drawings on the front to a later period, viz., the time when Mini entered Michelangelo's service, i.e. about 1523. I agree with this. (In the course of his long dissertation, however, he came to a different conclusion and dated the whole sheet about 1518-24, which I cannot accept.) I have given above the reasons for dating No. 34 about 1513; the date of No. 48 can be established by comparing it with No. 47, the latter being to a certain extent a preliminary study for the Madonna seen in profile, which I therefore date about 1523-24. As regards the pen technique, it should be compared with No. 53, which is of only slightly later date.

49. 'DAMNED SOUL' (A FURY). Black chalk. $11\frac{5}{8} \times 8$ in. Florence, Uffizi (No. 601E).

This is the most important of the three sheets which Michelangelo, according to Vasari, presented to Gherardo Perini (see under No. 47).

The Florence drawing was held to be a copy, and a version in Windor Castle the original, until Johannes Wilde (41, p. 264) established the correct relationship. There is a further copy in Florence.

At the top the drawing bears the inscription GHERARDUS DE PERINIS with the words MICHELAN. BONAROTI FACIEBAT below. Under this there are three intersected circles, Michelangelo's stonemason's mark (placed on all blocks of marble as soon as they had been purchased on his behalf at the quarries; see Fig. 5).

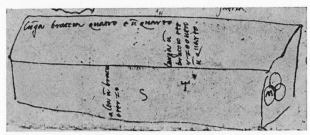

FIG. 5.—Michelangelo: sketch of a marble block, bearing his stonemason's mark; Florence, Archivio Buonarroti.

The head is usually called 'Anima Dannata', there being two grounds for this. Firstly, Michelangelo inserted an almost identical head in the 'Last Judgement', behind Minos; and secondly, Lorenzo Bernini called a very similar sculpture 'Testa di anima dannata'.[46] On the derivation of these works from a Medusa head, see my Excursus II, p. 177, and Plates 166, 167. The question arises, however, whether the correct designation would not be 'Furia'.

The following conjecture which, since I believed it for a long time, I present with the greatest confidence, must be taken with reserve, and if in the course of my remarks on the next sheet presented to Perini (No. 50), I make use of this conjecture as if it were a fact, the reader must nevertheless hold against me that it is nothing but a hypothesis.

In February, 1522—i.e. in the same month in which Michelangelo wrote the only letter to Gherardo Perini that has been preserved—there appeared the second edition of Ariosto's 'Orlando Furioso', the most important poem of the High Renaissance and a victory for Romanticism over Classicism.[47]

In the most impressive part of this poem madness is represented by love; indeed love itself is explained as being madness. I will quote a few passages:

'And when he found that he was all alone, with cries and groans opened the doors of grief./His eyes were sunken in his head, his face was pale and like a dried-up bone, his hair dishevelled, awesome and forbidding./I saw him . . . uttering fearsome howls and loud laments; he has gone mad./Various are the effects, but that wild madness which brings them out, is ever just the same. . . . And in conclusion I would say to you that he who, though old, still loves, the penalty deserves that he be bound and chained.' (XXIII, 124; XXIX, 60; XXXI, 45; XXIV, 2.) In addition to this, the poet says of himself that he has been gradually losing his reason since arrows from the eyes of his beloved have been piercing his heart (XXXV, 1).

Is it not legitimate to suppose that this screaming head was intended to be a symbol of Michelangelo's insane love for Gherardo Perini, since it is after all generally admitted that the Ganymede drawing symbolizes his love for Tommaso de' Cavalieri?

50. VENUS, MARS AND CUPID. Black chalk. $14\frac{1}{8} \times 9\frac{7}{8}$ in. Florence, Uffizi (No. 598E).

This is the third of the drawings presented to Gherardo Perini (cf. the text to Nos. 47 and 49). The only reason why its original purpose has been questioned by critics is the fact that the back of the sheet is covered with insignificant sketches by the hand of a pupil. Thode steadfastly maintained that it is authentic, despite the objections of Wölfflin, who had declared it to be a copy; of Morelli, who attributed it to Bacchiacca; and of Berenson, who for this drawing, too, suggested the name of 'Andrea'. Its authenticity has recently been defended once again by Johannes Wilde (41, p. 265).

There is a copy by Giulio Clovio at Windsor Castle, probably identical with the drawing mentioned in the 1577 inventory of Clovio's property as 'Il combattimento di Marte e Venere fatto da Do. Giulio et inventione di Michelagnolo'.[48] (Since the bearded head behind Venus wears a helmet, it probably does represent Mars, not Vulcan.)

The popular name for the drawing is 'Zenobia', but this was already discarded by Berenson and, on the basis of the Clovio copy, Johannes Wilde was able to point the way to the correct title.

Like the 'Furia' (No. 49), the drawing deals with the dark side of the realm of Venus, the 'sweet bitterness of love', as Sappho puts it. Here Venus appears, not smiling and persuasive, but armed, as she used to be represented in Sparta; her diadem has become a helmet, she is the armoured goddess, the consort of the blood spirit Mars, triumphing over all pride and all power. She is a fateful goddess who tears the lover out of his concealment, discipline and reverence and drives him on 'with the whip of Peitho'—Verticordia, who transforms not only hearts, but destinies, and leads them to fear, shame and destruction. Suidas said of her that she often appeared as a hermaphrodite.

About the same time as Michelangelo made this drawing, he created his marble group of 'The Victory'—a handsome young man triumphing over an old man crouching like a slave—a work which admits of the same erotic interpretation.

[46] In the church of Santa Maria di Monserrato, Rome (Photo, Anderson 17846).

[47] Ariosto, in the first edition of his 'Orlando Furioso' of 1516, had already made laudatory mention of Michelangelo's name.

[48] 'Battle between Mars and Venus, copy by Don Giulio Clovio after Michelangelo.'

It is surprising that the import of this drawing was not grasped during the Romantic period. Henry Fuseli drew a similar Venus Philomeda,[49] whose bosom is bound with the same high girdle as in Michelangelo's drawing, and whose countenance has the same mask-like stare; Aubrey Beardsley drew this terrible figure as Salome and as Lysistrata. Carl Justi came very near the truth when he said that the figure seemed to him to be a 'Bellona'.

The drawings of the 'Furia' and 'Venus and Mars', which Michelangelo presented to Gherardo Perini, thus seem to me to contain a confession, the language of which is even clearer than his most dolorous love-poems. Apart from their artistic value, these drawings have a special interest for modern psychologists.

51. THREE FEMALE PROFILES WITH FANTASTIC COIFFURES. Black chalk. 13⅜ × 9 in. Florence, Uffizi (No. 599E recto).

No. 47 is on the other side of the sheet, and what has been said above about it is also applicable to this drawing.

I date all the drawings presented to Gherardo Perini about 1522–23. In December, 1523, Antonio Mini entered Michelangelo's workshop, and although it does not make a continuance of the friendship with Perini impossible, the absence of any subsequent correspondence is striking. (But see note on No. 65.)

On the lower edge of the sheet we read in very blurred characters: 'Gherardo, io non o potuto oggi ve[nire]'—Gherardo, I could not come to-day.

52. YOUNG GIRL WITH DISTAFF. Black chalk. 11½ × 7¼ in. London, British Museum (1859-6-25-261).

Cursory, but unusually beautiful sketch; in its technique, e.g.

the long hatching lines, akin to Nos. 47 and 53; may be dated about 1524. Although Thode doubts its authenticity and Berenson attributes it to the assistant 'Andrea', the British Museum has very rightly placed it among the authentic drawings of Michelangelo.

The figure is seated on a high-backed chair or throne, her right arm and the distaff being merely indicated. The wide, decorative girdle and the ornaments on her bosom seem to point to her representing some antique personage—perhaps Arachne.

Formerly in the Casa Buonarroti.

53. TWO MADONNA SKETCHES. Pen and ink. 16 × 10⅝ in. London, British Museum (1859-5-14-818).

This sheet forms part of a group of pen-and-ink drawings (Nos. 53–58) illustrating the later style of Michelangelo in this technique.[50] The dating of this particular sheet is certain, since on the back, in Michelangelo's handwriting, there is a number of ricordi, or notes of payments made between the 4th and 8th October, 1524.[51] The contemporaneity of No. 53 with Nos. 54 and 55 was first demonstrated by A. E. Popp (20, p. 141).

No. 53 was 'probably drawn as a model for Antonio Mini', as Berenson puts it. Mini entered Michelangelo's workshop in December, 1523, at the age of seventeen, and remained there seven years. If we ignore all the drawings and paintings which Berenson, Popp and others have been only too willing to attribute to him, and consider only those drawings which can be proved to be his (see, e.g., Plate 207), Mini seems to have been one of the most ungifted artists who ever entered Michel-

---

[49] Paul Ganz, The Drawings of Henry Fuseli, Plate 81.

[50] For his early style in pen-and-ink technique, see Plates 1–24, dating from about 1492–1506; then the group dating from about 1513–14, Plates 31–36.

[51] A transcription and translation of these ricordi can be found in Fagan (27, p. 99 f.). See Fig. 6.

FIG. 6.—Ricordi in Michelangelo's handwriting, dated 1524; verso of Drawing No. 53.

angelo's entourage. At the bottom of the present drawing is an inscription in Michelangelo's handwriting: 'Disegna antonio disegna antonio, disegna e non perder tempo'—Draw, Antonio, draw, Antonio, draw and don't waste time! Antonio would thus seem to have spent his time in making clumsy copies of Michelangelo's pen-and-ink sketches.

The Madonna in profile is 'squared', i.e. covered with a quadrangular network of lines (which, as is well known, serve as an aid to the artist when he makes an enlargement or a cartoon).

Formerly in the Casa Buonarroti.

54. SKETCH FOR THE MEDICI MADONNA. Pen and ink. $15\frac{3}{8} \times 7\frac{5}{8}$ in. Vienna, Albertina (Cat. No. III, 132r).

A. E. Popp (20, p. 141) was the first to attempt to prove the contemporaneity of Nos. 54 and 53; Wickhoff (37, 152), without investigating the style, arrived at the same conclusion. Thode and Brinckmann dated it about 1504, the latter holding it to be a study for the Bruges Madonna. The first to deny its authenticity was Morelli; Baumgart (16, p. 48) gives exhaustive reasons in support of this, but I do not find them convincing. Tolnay (*The Sistine Ceiling*, 1945, p. 212) shares Baumgart's opinion.

On the back of the sheet is a nude study of a standing man, seen from behind, without arms, which is vaguely reminiscent of the studies for the Battle of Cascina; it is, however, nothing but an academic study by the hand of an anonymous assistant of Michelangelo's.

The question of the authenticity of No. 54 depends to no small extent on the dating. It would be idle to deny that the drawing has a certain stylistic resemblance to the sketches of Captives on No. 32, which can be dated 1513, to the figure of an Apostle on No. 35, which I date from the same time, and also to the drawing, made in 1514 (No. 36) for the Risen Christ. On the other hand, it would seem advisable to compare Nos. 53–58 once again with one another, in order to see whether the style of the latter group differs materially from that of the group first mentioned (the dating of 53, 57 and 58 being unquestioned). The chief difference—clearly shown by a comparison with No. 36—seems to be that the ductus of the pen has become far more calligraphic, the straight and curved hatching lines being arranged as if they were handwriting; moreover, it seems to me that the ductus in the pen-and-ink drawing we are discussing is far more similar to Michelangelo's handwriting about 1524 than it is to his writing about 1510–14. Assuming that one agrees with Thode, Brinckmann, Popp, Wilde, Popham and myself that the drawing is authentic, it remains to be decided whether it should be dated about 1513 (Berenson, Popham) or 1524 (Popp).

I myself (on the basis of the character of the pen strokes, which to me seem to be the same as in Nos. 53–58) follow Popp's dating, about 1524, and have no doubts as to the authenticity of any of the drawings in the whole group.

Formerly in the Mariette collection.

55. STUDIES FOR THE MEDICI MADONNA. Pen and ink. $10\frac{3}{4} \times 7\frac{5}{8}$ in. Paris, Louvre (No. 689).

See text to No. 54.

On the back of the sheet is a pen-and-ink drawing, a male nude seen from the front, probably by the hand of the same assistant who drew the study of a nude on the back of No. 54.

56. THIEF ON THE CROSS. Pen and ink. $9\frac{3}{4} \times 6\frac{1}{4}$ in. London, British Museum (1859-6-25-555).

Georg Gronau (*Mitteilungen des Kunsthistorischen Instituts in Florenz*, III, 1919, p. 38 f.) recognized that No. 56 belongs to the same period as Nos. 54 and 55. Tolnay, who denies that the drawing is by Michelangelo,[52] also rejects the old title ('Study for the Haman on the Sistine Chapel ceiling') and suggests the correct designation. The man on the left is standing among the branches of a tree, and the figure undoubtedly has some resemblance to one of the unfinished Boboli Captives, the so-called awaking giant.[53] The figure on the right, on the other hand, coincides with a bronze statuette in Berlin (Fig. 7a–b), which is attributed to Michelangelo and known as the 'Crucified Thief'.[54]

In my opinion the drawing can be dated by comparing it with Nos. 53–55 and 57–58, i.e. about 1524.

Formerly in the Casa Buonarroti.

57. THREE SKETCHES FOR A RIVER-GOD IN THE MEDICI CHAPEL. Pen and ink. $5\frac{1}{4} \times 8\frac{1}{4}$ in. London, British Museum (1859-6-25-544).

Frey recognized that these sketches are connected with the four river-gods which were to have been placed beneath the 'Phases of the Day'. Two of the sketches contain measurements. The third, in the right-hand lower corner, which is upside-down,

[52] Baumgart rejected Nos. 54 and 55, and Tolnay, agreeing with him on this point, had logically to exclude also No. 56. Bertini (15, p. 114) regards No. 56 as genuine but dates it about 1510–12.

[53] *Michelangelo's Sculptures*, Phaidon edition, 1950, Plate 73. The most characteristic feature of No. 56, the crossed right leg, appears in a very similar form in this figure of a Captive, but is lacking in the crucified Haman on the Sistine Chapel ceiling.

[54] Thode had already noticed the difference between the two figures in No. 56, and whereas he thinks that the figure on the left, standing 'on the stump of a hewn-off branch', like the crucified Haman in the spandrel fresco on the Sistine Chapel ceiling, is a study for this fresco, he says of the figure on the right that it has 'something of the poise of a Thief on the Cross'. On this point he anticipated Tolnay.

Thief on the Cross
FIG. 7a.—Michelangelo: detail of Drawing No. 56.
FIG. 7b.—After Michelangelo: bronze statuette (reversed) in the Berlin Museum.

has no measurements.[55] Michelangelo made the sketches with measurements about 1525, either for his own use or for the masons in Carrara. The river-gods were never executed in marble, as originally planned, but a large clay model of one of them is preserved in the Accademia at Florence.[56] This model was probably made for a river-god on the tomb of Lorenzo, but these pen-and-ink sketches, as A. E. Popp has demonstrated, must have been intended for another river-god, forming part of the tomb of Giuliano. We are indebted to Joseph Meder[57] for the observation that the sketches are all of the same figure, shown in different attitudes.

On the back of the sheet are parallel broken lines and a few words.

Formerly in the Casa Buonarroti.

58. LEG STUDY FOR A RECUMBENT FIGURE IN THE MEDICI CHAPEL. Pen and ink. 6 × 7½ in. Florence, Casa Buonarroti (No. 44F).

Anny E. Popp held that this drawing was a preliminary study for the 'Leda', made about 1530; to this Brinckmann made the amusing rejoinder that 'the tucked-in right foot of Leda would have made her inaccessible to the swan'.

Thode dated the sheet correctly about the time of the Medici tombs, and Brinckmann pointed out the resemblance to the statue of 'Night'. Thode thought that it was a sketch for a river-god. There is a *ricordo* on the back of the sheet, dated January 5, 1530; this late date supports Thode's view, since the river-gods were begun last of all the statues in the Medici Chapel.

59. SKETCH FOR THE 'DAY' IN THE MEDICI CHAPEL. Black chalk. 6¾ × 10⅝ in. Oxford, Ashmolean Museum (No. 7).

Several sketches in black chalk for the 'Phases of the Day' have been preserved; the authenticity of all of them has been doubted and is, in fact, doubtful. Their quality, however, is so high that I have reproduced two of them here. Brinckmann, Popp and Tolnay ignore these drawings, obviously because they consider them to be copies after the finished statues. Robinson has suggested that they may be drawings by Michelangelo after his own wax models. Berenson, Frey and Thode also believe that this and the following drawing are authentic, and date them about 1525.

Formerly in the Reynolds and Lawrence collections.

60. SKETCH FOR THE 'NIGHT' IN THE MEDICI CHAPEL. Black chalk. 6½ × 11¼ in. London, British Museum (1859-6-25-569 *recto*).

See the text to No. 59.

Drawn from a male model, although intended for a female statue. (Cf. No. 30.)

On the back of the sheet is a walking male nude, seen from the back.

Formerly in the Casa Buonarroti.

61. STUDY FOR A PIETÀ. Black chalk. 15¾ × 11 in. Florence, Casa Buonarroti (No. 69F).

Berenson thought that this was a preliminary study for No. 43 and dated both drawings about 1510, the time of the work on the Sistine Chapel ceiling. Panofsky (*Festschrift für Julius von Schlosser*, 1927, p. 150 f.) took the sketches on the back as his starting-point and dated the whole sheet from the time of the 'Last Judgement', i.e. about 1534. But of the seven sketches on the back (Photo Brogi 1347-C) none are by Michelangelo. Thode had already pointed out 'that the arm on this sheet reminds us of many of the arms in the "Last Judgement"'—e.g. the arm of Christ is similar, although inverted as if seen in a mirror. No. 61, or a similar drawing, was used for the sleeping soldier at the utmost right in No. 78.

In my opinion this drawing is not earlier, but later, than No. 43 (see also the text to No. 43). The technique is already close to that of the drawings of the 1530's, e.g. Nos. 78 and 83, but it is even closer to that of Nos. 59 and 60, though it is true that the authenticity of both these drawings is doubtful. I date it about 1525-30 and do not think that it is a copy (cf. Dussler, *Sebastiano del Piombo*, p. 188).

62. WRESTLERS. Black chalk. 4½ × 3¾ in. Haarlem, Teyler Museum (No. 21B).

Two (doubtful) sketches for the same group in London and Oxford (BB. 1490 and 1712) seem to me to be much weaker than this drawing, the authenticity of which is rejected by the more recent critics, with the exception of Berenson and Thode. The drawings in London and Oxford are called 'Hercules and Antaeus'.

In a letter written in October, 1525 (Frey, 260), Michelangelo complained that the Pope wanted to give to Bandinelli the block of marble destined for a marble group representing one of the feats of Hercules;[58] Bandinelli eventually received the block of marble. The sculpture was planned as a counterpart to Michelangelo's 'David' in front of the entrance to Palazzo Vecchio in Florence. Michelangelo subsequently used his sketches of the 'Hercules and Antaeus' for a somewhat altered clay model of 'Samson Slaying the Philistines', which has been preserved in the Casa Buonarroti.[59] In the drawing we are discussing Michelangelo has transformed the subject once again; here, as Thode was the first to notice, the abduction of a woman is represented, either the Rape of a Sabine Woman or the Rape of Proserpina. Giovanni Bologna used Michelangelo's composition for his well-known Rape of the Sabines in the Loggia dei Lanzi (terra-cotta model in the Accademia at Florence). It is a striking fact that Giovanni Bologna also used the same idea for a small bronze representing 'Hercules and Antaeus' (L. Planiscig, *Piccoli Bronzi*, 1930, Fig. 359). On the back of the sheet the outlines have been traced—'probably by a later hand', as Berenson observes.

63. SKETCH FOR A DECORATIVE MASK. Red and black chalk. 9¾ × 4¾ in. Windsor Castle, Royal Library (Inv. No. 12762). Sketched in red chalk and executed in black chalk. To judge by the style, about 1530.

Silvio Cosini's frieze of masks behind the 'Phases of the Day' in the Medici chapel shows only a superficial resemblance to

---

[55] The ductus in this figure, especially as regards the right arm, in so far as it is drawn, coincides exactly with that of the seated women in No. 55.

[56] *Michelangelo's Sculptures*, Phaidon edition, 1950, Plate 114.

[57] *Die Handzeichnung*, 2nd edition, 1923, p. 366, Meder is speaking only of two sketches; the third, in the right bottom corner, has hitherto been overlooked.

[58] The choice lay between two subjects—Hercules and Cacus, or Hercules and Antaeus.

[59] *Michelangelo's Sculptures*, Phaidon edition, 1950, Plate 118. This composition was freely copied by Giovanni Bologna in a large group in the Musée Municipal at Douai (Photo Bulloz).

this drawing; one of the two capital masks to the right of the statue of Lorenzo de' Medici is more closely related to it; it should, however, be compared with the mask on the back of the Giuliano,[60] in which the headgear and the two drops beneath the chin are found as they are in the sketch. This mask was probably executed by Montorsoli (Milanesi, *Les Correspondants de Michel-Ange*, I, 114), perhaps after this sketch, which in the course of the execution was simplified and coarsened.

Johannes Wilde has pointed out that No. 63 was used again thirty years later for the lunette mask on the Porta Pia.

On the back of the sheet are sketches by the hand of a pupil, whom one can without misgivings identify as Antonio Mini. The latter left Michelangelo towards the end of 1531 and went to France and died there in 1533.

A similar headgear is found in the Leda cartoon (Plate 173), and this, too, points to the year 1530.

Plate 63 reproduces only the upper part of the sheet; the lower half, which virtually contains nothing, has been omitted.

64. DESIGNS FOR SMALL SCULPTURES. Soft black chalk. $6\frac{1}{8} \times 6\frac{1}{4}$ in. Cambridge (Mass.), The Fogg Museum of Art (No. 1932–152).

The fantastic head of an animal in the upper right corner was probably intended as a model for a lamp. There are two similar bronze lamps by Riccio in the Museo Estense at Modena (Bode, *Bronzestatuetten*, small edition, 1922, Plate 55). The faun, below on the left, with a hod on its shoulders, is likewise a model for a lamp, or perhaps for a small censer. Another lamp by Riccio, in the Museo Nazionale, Florence, is more or less a combination of these two sketches of Michelangelo's—it consists of a fantastic animal's head with a boy crouching on top of it (Bode, *op. cit.*, Plate 54).

---

[60] *The Sculptures of Michelangelo*, Phaidon edition, 1950, Plate 87.

On the same sheet are also four slighter sketches. Below, on the right: an eye and a man with his head between the horns of a lyre; below, on the left: a man with raised right arm (reminiscent of background figures in No. 93); above on the left: a woman with head thrown back and arms raised in lament (similar to one of the figures in No. 94).

A kindred drawing by Michelangelo, of somewhat later date, in the British Museum (formerly in the Oppenheimer collection), shows a design for a richly ornamented vessel with a lid.

No. 64 has passed through various well-known collections, among them those of Jonathan Richardson, Lord Spencer and Charles Loeser.

65. PROFILE WITH FANTASTIC HEAD-DRESS. Red chalk. $8\frac{1}{8} \times 6\frac{5}{8}$ in. Oxford, Ashmolean Museum (No. 10).

This drawing, judged by its style, belongs to the same group as those presented to Perini (Nos. 49–51), but the manner has here become more mechanical—similar to No. 64, so that I date it towards the close of the period, about 1528–30.

The drawings presented to Perini were attributed by Morelli to Bacchiacca, and the same writer and Loeser added several other drawings to the group, among these being the sheet in Frankfurt (Berenson, Figs. 775 and 784), the two heads in the Uffizi (Berenson, Fig. 783), the so-called Count of Canossa and the so-called Marchesa di Pescara in the British Museum (Berenson, Figs. 780 and 786).[61] Berenson attributes all these drawings to his 'Andrea di Michelangelo'. They are of uneven quality, and I believe that we can here draw a distinction between Michelangelo's originals and drawings of similar content made by an imitator. Authentic are the three drawings for Perini, the 'Marchesa di Pescara' (BB. 1689) and the

---

[61] Morelli, in *Kunstchronik*, new series, III (1891–92) and IV (1892–93). Loeser, in *Archivio Storico dell'Arte*, new series, III, p. 352 f.

Heads with fantastic Turbans

FIG. 8.—Michelangelo: detail of Drawing No. 65. Oxford, Ashmolean Museum.

FIG. 9.—Bacchiacca: Salome, detail of a painting in the Berlin Museum.

drawing we are discussing. As regards the remainder, I follow Morelli's opinion; Bacchiacca frequently used similar heads in his paintings. No. 65 differs more markedly in quality from the latter than a copy normally does from its original, and the attribution to Bacchiacca (Tolnay, No. 15–A) is acceptable only if one also rejects the three presentation drawings for Perini, which are among Michelangelo's best achievements; this has actually been done, but quite wrongly. It should be noted that the most important argument in favour of such an attribution is the fact that Bacchiacca used this or a similar head for his Salome in the 'Beheading of John the Baptist' (see Fig. 9 on p. 41).[62]

The only genuine Bacchiacca drawing that might be compared with this one is a red chalk study in the Albertina (BB.189, reproduced by A. E. Popham in *Italian Drawings*, Oxford, 1931, Plate 199–B); here, too, the figure is turned in such a way that we can see the back, but the head is in profile. Despite all this external resemblance, Bacchiacca's completely different technique stands out—his superficiality, his lack of plastic feeling, his striving after elegance and decorative values.

Anny Popp (in *Belvedere*, VIII, Forum, p. 75) ascribes No. 65 to a pupil of Michelangelo named 'Carlo', and believes that the drawing is a free copy of the slave on the left above the Prophet Joel.[63] In my opinion this theory of Popp's leads to only one positive result, namely, that the model was a young man, as were the models for the Captives, and not a woman (cf. Nos. 30 and 60).[64]

Formerly in the Casa Buonarroti and the Wicar and Lawrence collections.

66. HEAD STUDY FOR THE 'LEDA'. Red chalk. $14 \times 10\frac{5}{8}$ in. Florence, Casa Buonarroti (No. 7F).

This drawing has always been assigned to the period of the Sistine Chapel ceiling frescoes, and dated about 1508–11. Berenson was reminded of the Libyan Sibyl; Steinmann, Venturi, Brinckmann and Tolnay, of a figure in the Ozias spandrel fresco; Thode of a female head in the Manasses and Amon lunette. Its real purpose was first established by Johannes Wilde (41, p. 247); the head is a study for the Leda cartoon.

In the summer of 1529, when Michelangelo went to Ferrara during the siege of Florence, he promised to make a painting

for Duke Alfonso I d'Este. Condivi relates the story in detail in the fortieth paragraph of his biography of Michelangelo. In the autumn of 1530 the painting was finished—'a large chamber-picture, representing Leda lying with the Swan, and nearby the birth of the egg, from which Castor and Pollux were born; as may be read, written in the fables of the ancients'; to which Vasari adds: 'a certain large picture, delicately painted in tempera'. The envoy sent by the Duke to fetch the picture behaved very tactlessly and offended Michelangelo (as we read in Condivi and Vasari), who refused to hand over the painting. A year later he presented it to his pupil Antonio Mini, before the latter's departure for France, together with the cartoon. Mini opened a workshop in Lyons for the production of copies of the 'Leda', his partner Benedetto del Bene apparently doing most of the work. Vasari asserts that in 1568 Michelangelo's 'Leda' was in Fontainebleau,[65] whereas the cartoon had been sent back to Florence and was in the possession of Bernardo Vecchietti. It seems, however, certain that the Fontainebleau picture is identical with the copy on canvas in London (National Gallery, No. 1868), which is now generally considered to have been painted by Rosso Fiorentino.

The copy of the eye and nose, below on the left, is (as Brinckmann has pointed out) in a lighter-coloured red chalk and is the work of an assistant—but not of Mini.

67. SAMSON AND DELILAH. Red chalk. $10\frac{5}{8} \times 15\frac{1}{2}$ in. Oxford, Ashmolean Museum (No. 55).

At one time wrongly attributed to Montelupo[66] and Mini; mentioned by Johannes Wilde (41, p. 250) among the authentic drawings and described as a 'presentation sheet'.

The stylistic relationship of this drawing to the two following, Nos. 68 and 69, strikes the eye. It has already been correctly dated 1530 by Thode and Berenson.

There is a partial copy of this drawing, by Antonio Mini, at Windsor Castle (Cat. 425 *verso*), and a similar drawing by the same weak hand at Oxford, which makes the attribution of No. 67 to Mini incomprehensible.

This composition[67] was the immediate source of another,[68] namely, a 'Venus and Cupid'. This (lost) cartoon was made by Michelangelo about 1532 for his friend Bartolomeo Bettini and was at one time in the collection of Duke Cosimo I de' Medici in Florence, to a certain extent as a counterpart to the 'Leda' cartoon (No. 66).

No. 67 was formerly in the Casa Buonarroti and the Wicar and Lawrence collections.

---

[62] Of this Michelangelo drawing there are two copies—one in the Ashmolean Museum, attributed to Salviati or alternatively to Battista Franco; the other, in the Uffizi, seems to me to coincide in technique with BB. 1688, 1630 and 1669, for which reason I think that it is a copy by the hand of Bacchiacca.

[63] *The Paintings of Michelangelo*, second Phaidon edition, London, 1948, Plate 47. Michelangelo often returned to old motives, as I point out on various other occasions in this book.

[64] At this point I would like to bring forward a supposition which cannot be proved. Twice in his life Michelangelo made portraits of young men—Tommaso de' Cavalieri, 'in a cartoon in life size', as Vasari informs us; and Cecchino Bracci, as we learn from a letter written by Luigi del Riccio in August, 1554: 'I beseech you, try to find again a certain drawing of which I have already spoken to you, so that you may carve the head of Cecchino from it.' If we admit the relationship of No. 65 to the presentation drawings for Perini, then we may suspect that the model for this head was Perini himself.

The Danish poet, Jens Peter Jacobsen—who knew only the copy in the Uffizi—in his poem entitled 'Arabesque on a drawing by Michelangelo', senses the erotic atmosphere pervading this drawing, and writes: '*That is innocence, enchanted by thy glance,/which seeth not, yet wildly sucks/the stormy flood of the veins' red stream,/ as the moon sucks up the ocean's frigid water . . . /Mighty blind Maenad,/ strange waves glitter in the darkness and foam with strange sounds . . ./ and the full-throated bellowing of madness.*'

[65] K. Kusenberg, *Le Rosso*, Paris, 1931, p. 45 f. The cartoon in the Royal Academy, London (Plate 173), is also by Rosso. The numerous copies of the 'Leda' to be found in various collections are inferior to the two in London.

[66] Montelupo was left-handed and his drawings are therefore easily distinguished; like the drawings of Leonardo and Holbein, they have hatching lines running from top left to bottom right.

[67] The motives in this drawing can be linked up with other compositions by Michelangelo, viz.: (a) the river-gods for the Medici chapel; (b) the river-gods of the 'Phaëthon' (Nos. 94 and 96); (c) the sketches for 'Hercules and Cacus' and 'David and Goliath' (Nos. 105–107); (d) the figure of Samson is almost exactly repeated in the chief figure of the 'Dream of Human Life' (No. 93), except that in No. 93, on account of the sitting position, one leg is hanging down; (e) the curious position of Samson's arms—one arm supported at a right angle, the other lying across the breast—is found again in a very similar form in Nos. 62 and 72, and in the figure raising the lid of the sarcophagus (No. 78). This is a good example of how Michelangelo exploited a motive to the limit.

[68] See Plate 150.

68. THREE LABOURS OF HERCULES. Red chalk. 10¾ × 16⅝ in. Windsor Castle, Royal Library (Inv. No. 12770).

Presentation drawing for an unknown friend, about 1530. The subjects are: the slaying of the Nemean lion, the wrestling match with Antaeus, and the fight with the Lernaean Hydra.[69] The authenticity of the drawing has been doubted by Anny Popp, who considers it to be a forgery, and by Erwin Panofsky, who thinks it is a copy.

It is one of Michelangelo's most important drawings, and symbolizes the virtue of the 'Vita activa'.

In Cristoforo Landino's 'Quaestiones Camaldulenses',[70] one of the speakers, Lorenzo de' Medici, mentions Hercules as the representative of the Active Life: 'Wise was Hercules, but he was not wise for his own sake alone, but helped mankind with his wisdom. On his wanderings, which led him over the greater part of the earth, he destroyed loathsome beasts, slew dangerous monsters, subdued dreadful tyrants, and restored law and liberty to many a nation. . . . Had he devoted all his labour to idle wisdom, he would have stood before us as a sophist, instead of a hero, and none would venture to call him the son of Jupiter, who likewise, in so far as we, following the Platonists, can hold him to be an earthly soul, is never idle. For if he were so, then would everything that is in constant movement cease to move: the heavens would no longer accomplish their eternal orbits, the stars would no longer rise and set, and the elements would no longer mingle and be transformed.'

The three parts of this drawing—the struggles with the lion, the giant and the nine-headed Hydra—correspond with the three categories of deeds for which Hercules is praised in Landino's dialogue—the overcoming of beasts, evil men and monsters.

69. RUNNING SATYR. Black chalk. 10⅜ × 7 in. Paris, Louvre (No. 707).

Classified by Johannes Wilde among the authentic drawings (41, p. 248), as a study for the figure with a bow in the upper left corner of No. 73; Berenson arrived at the same conclusion. The divergences between the two figures are considerable, e.g. in the position of the right arm.

Beneath the raised foot is a sketch of an ornament;[71] on the right edge of the sheet, a sketch of a hip. About 1530.

Formerly in the Coypel collection.

70. STUDY FOR THE 'NOLI ME TANGERE'. Black chalk. 10½ × 7⅝ in. Florence, Casa Buonarroti (No. 45 F).

Hitherto this study has been held to be a sketch for the Sistine Chapel fresco of the 'Expulsion of Adam from the Garden of Eden', but the style of the draughtsmanship is very different from Michelangelo's manner about 1508. (Besides, the drawing is executed in artificial chalk, which Michelangelo does not appear to have used before about 1530.)

The motive of the body, however, is derived from the above-mentioned fresco. Michelangelo made use of this motive on three further occasions—in the cartoon of the 'Noli me tangere' (1531),[72] in the 'Christ and the Woman of Samaria' for Vittoria Colonna (1542),[73] and in the 'Christ taking leave of His Mother' (about 1555).[74]

The painting of the 'Noli me tangere' was commissioned at the beginning of 1531 by Alfonso Davalos, Marchese di Guasto, a general in the imperial army, through the good offices of Nicolaus von Schomberg, Archbishop of Capua and Governor of Florence. From a letter written by Figiovanni to the Master (Frey, 48, p. 507; dated April 11, 1531) we learn that Michelangelo was first to produce a 'schizzo di carbone', i.e. a charcoal sketch or cartoon. The cartoon was finished in the late summer of 1531, and after it Pontormo painted two panels in oil colours; another copy was made by Battista Franco (Plate 140). The cartoon was at one time in the art collection of Duke Cosimo I de' Medici (who also owned the cartoons of the 'Leda' and the 'Venus and Cupid') in Florence, but has since been lost.

The present sketch was used in the cartoon only for the turning of the bodies and arms, but both arms were shown more lowered. A second sketch, No. 71, shows the recoiling poise of the whole figure, as in the cartoon, but the arms are in quite a different position.[75] Michelangelo's cartoon (to judge from Franco's copy) bore a certain resemblance to Dürer's woodcuts of 'Christ taking leave of His Mother' (B. 21 and 92).

71. STUDY FOR THE 'NOLI ME TANGERE'. Red chalk. 9 × 3¼ in. Florence, Casa Buonarroti (No. 62 F).

In his sketch for the Christ (No. 70), Michelangelo adhered

---

[69] The three groups in this drawing are derived from sculptures. A bronze by Michelangelo's teacher Bertoldo (about 1480) in the Victoria and Albert Museum shows the upper body and arms of Hercules in the struggle with the lion in the same position as in Michelangelo's drawing (reproduced by Planiscig in *Piccoli Bronzi*, Milan, 1930, Plate XI, Fig. 16). The middle group has two different sources. First, an antique cameo, 'Hercules fighting with Antaeus' (Furtwängler, *Antike Gemmen*, Plate XXVII, 15), and an antique marble group in the Uffizi, formerly in the Belvedere (Hekler, *Michelangelo und die Antike*, p. 222). Secondly, as far as the composition itself is concerned, it has been developed out of an Etruscan cameo (e.g. Lippold, *Gemmen und Kameen*, Plate XXXVII, 2); this cameo in its turn is derived from Greek coins (G. F. Hill, *Select Greek Coins*, Plate XLVII, 3 and 5), and was repeatedly copied by the creators of Renaissance plaques. For purposes of comparison I would also mention 'Nike killing an Ox', until 1527 in the Palazzo della Valle (now in Munich). The third group is, as Frey was the first to notice, derived from the Laocoön. Similar to Mantegna's engraving (B. XIII, 11), which Michelangelo is also held to have taken as a model, is a sketch by Dürer of Hercules slaying the Nemean lion, made about 1511 (Lippmann 765, Winkler 491), but there the figures are turned more towards the left; the composition is almost identical with Dürer's woodcut of 'Samson killing the Lion' (B. 2).

[70] *Landini Quaestiones Camaldulenses ad Federicum Urbinatum Principem*, Florentiae, c. 1470. In these dialogues, after Hercules, 'the men who have propagated the Christian faith', i.e. the Apostles and, above all, St. Paul, are exalted as representatives of the Active Life. The same may be said both of Hercules and St. Paul, viz., that they fought against evil and journeyed 'over the greater part of the earth'. The problem of the Vita Activa also engaged the attention of Cardinal Pole, with whom Michelangelo came into contact at the time when the Cardinal, as administrator of the Patrimonium Petri, was residing at Viterbo (after 1541; at the same time as Vittoria Colonna). This contact with Cardinal Pole is confirmed by Condivi, who writes: 'He (Michelangelo) has therefore gladly entertained the friendship of those from whose virtuous and learned conversation he might draw some profit, and through whom he might reflect some ray of excellence: as of the very reverend and illustrious Monsignor Pole, for his rare virtues and singular goodness.' In Thomas Starkey's 'Dialogue' (written about 1534) a conversation between Cardinal Pole and Thomas Lupset is quoted, in the course of which the Cardinal gives his opinion on the conflict arising from the choice between the Vita Contemplativa and the Vita Activa; in the end he decides in favour of the Vita Activa. (W. Schenk, *Reginald Pole*, London, 1950, p. 32 f., p. 77; Starkey's *Dialogue*, ed. Miss J. M. Cowper, 1948).

[71] The only more or less exhaustive description of Michelangelo's ornaments appeared in the nineteenth special number of the *Jahrbuch der kunsthistorischen Sammlungen in Wien*, new series, 1928; it is by Frida Schottmüller and is entitled *Michelangelo und die Ornamentik*.

[72] Plate 140.

[73] Plate 139.

[74] Plate 119.

[75] In his studies for the 'Christ taking Leave of His Mother', Michelangelo returned to the motives of the two studies, Nos. 70 and 71; see Plates 119a and b.

more or less to the movement of the Adam in the 'Expulsion from the Garden of Eden', though in this sketch he expresses not only Christ's shrinking back, but also his recoil, for the upper part of the body is inclined backwards and the left arm is raised in a warding-off gesture. The cartoon (Plate 140) shows a partial return to the original idea.

There is yet a third sketch for this figure of Christ in the Archivio Buonarroti (Tolnay, No. 103). In this third version the upper part of the body is thrown back still further, but the left arm, the most impressive feature in No. 71, is omitted. Tolnay holds that the drawing under discussion is a copy of his No. 103, but disregards the important differences. Anny Popp, without cognizance of the red chalk sketch in the Archivio Buonarroti, believed that our drawing was only a copy (20, p. 162), while Berenson attributed it to Mini; these critics relate the sketch to the soldier with a shield in No. 79. Frey and Thode admit the authenticity of the drawing, and so does Johannes Wilde (41, p. 249), who describes it as a study for the 'Noli me tangere'; Thode aptly remarks that the figure has 'merely a general' relationship to the terrified soldier in No. 79.

72. STUDY FOR A BACKGROUND FIGURE IN THE 'RISEN CHRIST'. Red chalk. 5¼ × 8⅜ in. Florence, Casa Buonarroti (No. 32F).

Used in Nos. 77 and 78 for the soldier raising the lid of the sarcophagus (cf. Wilde, 41, p. 251). Developed in an inverted form from No. 67. The body motive coincides fairly exactly with that of the Ananias in Raphael's figured tapestry in the Vatican.

73. ARCHERS SHOOTING AT A HERM. Red chalk. 8⅝ × 12¾ in. Windsor Castle, Royal Library (Inv. No. 12778).

Goethe[76] (who, be it noted, did not know the original, but saw only the fresco copy which was then in the Villa Raffaele) understood the import of this work and described it as 'a mysterious, allegorical picture, probably depicting the power of the fleshly lusts'. In this case the figure of Herm, protected by a shield, would symbolize the soul. In a sonnet by Michelangelo (Frey, CXIX) we read: 'Chè l'alma, quasi giunta all'altra riva/Fa scudo a' tuo' di più pietosi strali'—'the soul, which has all but reached the further bank, is as a shield against the most fervent arrows of Love.' Conze, Thode and Panofsky quote passages from Lucian, Cristoforo Landino, Mario Equicola and Pico della Mirandola, in their efforts to explain the drawing.[77] Many elements in the drawing have remained unexplained. It contains, among other figures, five putti, one of whom has wings and is lying asleep by his quiver; except for the faun, above on the left,[78] he is the only member of the group who has a bow; two more putti are hardening the points of their arrows (or burning the arrows?), and two others are running with the adults, two of whom are female and six male; two further figures are lying on the ground, one of them with hand raised in astonishment. Has it not some significance that the only winged putto takes no part in the action, but is asleep? Is there no meaning in the fact that not a single arrow has wounded the Herm, but that all have remained impaled in the shield, the mantle or the socle? or in the fact that the attackers have no bows? If we take Goethe's brief explanation as a starting-point, we arrive at the conclusion that against the soul, which is able to protect itself, all the passions are powerless.

On the back of the sheet is a memorandum dated April 12, 1530, and a note to the effect that the drawing was in the possession of Giulio Clovio; according to Johannes Wilde this also proves that it was not a presentation drawing for Tommaso de' Cavalieri. The note on the back ('D. Giulio Clovio copia di Michiel Angelo') induced Anny Popp to reject the drawing as being a copy by Clovio; Panofsky and Tolnay agree that it is only a copy. Johannes Wilde, however, has demonstrated its authenticity in a convincing manner.[79]

A copy of this drawing by Bernardino Cesari (in the same collection, Cat. No. 456) reproduces it in its entirety, i.e. before it was cut on all four sides.

Formerly in the collections of Giulio Clovio and Cardinal Alessandro Farnese.

74. TITYUS. Black chalk. 7½ × 13 in. Windsor Castle, Royal Library (Inv. No. 12771).

Tityus, the giant son of Terra, fell in love with Latona, mother of Apollo and Diana. He attempted to do violence to her, but she summoned to her aid her children, who slew him with their arrows. He was cast into hell, where vultures perpetually fed upon his liver. Virgil mentions him in the *Aeneid* (VI, 595 f.): 'Likewise one might see Tityus, nursling of the Earth, the universal mother. Over nine full acres his body is stretched, and a monstrous vulture with crooked beak gnaws at his deathless liver and vitals fruitful for anguish; deep within the breast he lodges and gropes for his feast; nor is any respite given to the filaments that grow anew.' Ovid (*Metamorphoses*, IV, 457 f.) also devotes a few lines to the sufferings of Tityus, but Michelangelo's immediate source was perhaps only the short 55th fable of Hyginus.

Lucretius, in the third canto of his *De Rerum Natura*, says that the image of Tityus whose body is devoured by vultures must be interpreted as that of a man whose heart is continually torn by the pangs of love—'the pangs of a shameful amorous desire', as he says in amplification. Thus interpreted, No. 74 would form a counterpart to Nos. 49 and 50. Tityus is the symbol of the penalty for illicit love.

According to Dante (*Inferno*, XXXII) the sons of Terra, among them Tityus, are in hell because they rebelled against the gods, and they are thus in the same position as heretics. In one of Savonarola's sermons we read: 'The sexual urge directs all the senses towards corporeal things. Do not therefore wonder that the lascivious become unbelievers . . . but there is no better remedy for sexual obsession than religious contemplation.'

This drawing thus represents not only the tortures of a lover, but the sin and its penalty, the punishment for a wanton desire which leads to the greater sin of defection from God.

No. 74 is a presentation drawing made for Tommaso de' Cavalieri, whose acquaintance Michelangelo made during the winter of 1532, and to whom he sent love-poems, drawings and letters; their relationship lasted until the end of Michelangelo's life. In December, 1532, at a time when Tommaso was ill, Michelangelo sent him by the hand of the sculptor Pierantonio

---

[76] *Reisejournal*, under March 14, 1788.
[77] There is a good conspectus of the literature on the subject in *Antike und Renaissance* by Arnold von Salis, Zürich, 1947, p. 241.
[78] No. 69 is a study for this figure.

[79] A. E. Popham (*Master Draughtsmen*, No. 1, London, 1930, Plate 11) likewise upholds the authenticity of the drawing.

Cecchini a letter and two drawings—the 'Tityus' and the 'Ganymede'. Tommaso answered him in a letter dated January 1, 1533: 'I hope . . . that in a few days I shall be restored to health and that I shall be able to visit you, should that be agreeable to you. Meanwhile I will comfort myself by contemplating for at least two hours a day your two drawings which Pierantonio brought me and which give me ever greater pleasure, the longer I look at them.'

The 'Ganymede' drawing has been lost and is preserved only in the form of a copy by the hand of Giulio Clovio (Windsor Castle, Cat. No. 457). The counterpart to the mental anguish of Tityus is Ganymede's flight to heaven; we may remember a passage from one of Michelangelo's sonnets to Cavalieri: 'If one spirit, one will but dominates two hearts,/If one soul makes itself immortal in two bodies/And bears them up to heaven on one wing'.[80]

Vasari (VII, p. 271) gives a list of the drawings presented by Michelangelo to Tommaso de' Cavalieri: 'More than to all the others and with the greatest tenderness was Michelangelo drawn towards the Roman nobleman Tommaso de' Cavalieri. The latter was still young and loved art. Wherefore, in order to instruct him in drawing, Michelangelo presented him with a number of most magnificent pages, among them divinely beautiful heads done in black and red chalk. He gave him also a Ganymede, whom the bird carries away to Zeus, a Tityus, whose heart the vulture is tearing out, and furthermore a fall of Phaëthon with his sun chariot into the Po and a Bacchanal of Children; each single page was admirable and drawn with rare art such as was never seen before. Michelangelo also made a portrait of Tommaso, a cartoon in life size—the only portrait he ever created. . . . Ser Tommaso took such delight in these drawings that Michelangelo also gave him a number of others, originally destined for Sebastiano Veneziano, that he might execute them in colours. They are wonderful and Tommaso preserves them like relics; yet he is most friendly in allowing artists access to them.'[81]

At the time of the Tityus drawing Michelangelo was working on the composition of the 'Risen Christ'. This becomes clear if we examine the sketches on the back of the 'Tityus'; the sheet was held against the light and the outlines of the Tityus were traced on the back, in such a way as to produce a standing figure, looking like a first sketch for No. 81; the sarcophagus and its lid were then indicated by a few lines.

Formerly in the collections of Tommaso de' Cavalieri and Cardinal Alessandro Farnese.

[80] The question still remains whether the *Ganymede* may not have a second, Christian mystic meaning, in relation to that passage from the Revelation of St. John (xii. 14) which Botticelli also illustrated and certified by means of an inscription (London, National Gallery, No. 1034). In this passage we read that to the Mother of God were given the wings of an eagle that she might fly into the wilderness and escape the persecution of the Devil. Ganymede is borne up to heaven by the eagle just as 'the woman which brought forth the man child' saved him from Satan, who 'was cast out into the earth'. Interpreted in this sense, the alternative title for the Ganymede drawing would be 'Deliverance from Sin'. Sebastiano del Piombo already connected the *Ganymede* with the Revelation of St. John—in a letter to Michelangelo, dated 17 July, 1533 (Milanesi, *Les Correspondants*, p. 106): 'One could draw a halo round the head of Ganymede, to make him appear as St. John of the Revelation, carried up to heaven.' For the erotic meaning of the *Ganymede*, cf. Ludwig von Scheffler, *Michelangelo: eine Renaissancestudie*, Altenburg, 1892, p. 53; or the more detailed study by E. Panofsky in *Studies in Iconology*, New York, 1939, p. 218. In 1531 Alciati's 'Emblemata' appeared in print for the first time; in this volume a woodcut of Prometheus coincides more or less with the Tityus; another woodcut and aphorism refer to Ganymede, and there is also a Phaëthon.

[81] See Plates 92, 94-96.

75. MOVEMENT STUDY FOR THE 'RISEN CHRIST'. Black chalk. $14\frac{3}{8} \times 9\frac{1}{2}$ in. Florence, Casa Buonarroti (No. 61 F).

The sketch on the front of this sheet (Brinckmann 61) has been reproduced time after time; according to Steinmann and Thode it is a study for the 'Risen Christ'; according to Brinckmann, a study for Christ the Judge in the 'Last Judgement' in the Sistine Chapel.

The back of the sheet, here reproduced for the first time,[82] makes it clear that here and in a similar drawing (Brinckmann, 62; BB. 1167) we have to do with sketches for the 'Risen Christ'.

From the summer of 1532 until the end of the year (cf. No. 74 *verso*), and perhaps even longer, Michelangelo worked on several versions of the 'Risen Christ' and on the similar composition of 'Christ in Limbo' (cf. No. 80). The motive of the present sketch is not repeated either in No. 78 or in No. 79, in which the right arm is stretched out and the left arm raised. The present drawing is interesting because it is one of the few sketches by Michelangelo that have been preserved which represents a spontaneous first draft, giving nothing but the movement.

It was obviously this lack of definite form that led Berenson to consider it to be the work of a pupil.

76. STUDY FOR THE 'RISEN CHRIST'. Black chalk. $16\frac{1}{2} \times 11\frac{3}{4}$ in. Florence, Casa Buonarroti (No. 65 *verso*).

A sketch for this drawing, but inverted and with the raised arm differently poised, is to be found on the back of a letter from Bartolomeo Angiolini, dated September 19, 1532 (Archivio Buonarroti, Cod. VI, fol. 24; reproduced by Tolnay, 21, Fig. 160). On the other side of No. 76 is a general design for the 'Last Judgement' (No. 100; about 1534). No. 76 was, in fact, used for several figures of the 'Last Judgement', with minor alterations.[83]

The body motive in No. 76 represents a return to older motives (cf. Nos. 17 and 20).

Tolnay thinks that this drawing is a copy, but this assumption has already been refuted by Berenson and Johannes Wilde.

77. THE RISEN CHRIST. Red chalk. $6\frac{1}{4} \times 6\frac{3}{4}$ in. Paris, Louvre (Inv. No. 691b).

Sketch for the following drawing, No. 78.

Formerly in the Jabach, Coypel and Robert de Cotte collections.

78. THE RISEN CHRIST. Black chalk. $9\frac{1}{2} \times 13\frac{5}{8}$ in. Windsor Castle, Royal Library (Inv. No. 12767).

Popp (20, p. 162) advances the hypothesis that this drawing was intended for a lunette fresco on the entrance wall of the Medici chapel. In her opinion, No. 77 is of later date than the drawing we are discussing. Such theories can hardly be accepted.

The date of the drawing is 1532-33 (cf. the text to No. 75).

On the back of the sheet are studies of masks, which Popp attributes to Giulio Clovio, the former owner of the drawing.

[82] See Johannes Wilde, 41, p. 251, under No. 428.

[83] Tolnay (21, p. 104) relates No. 76 to a similar drawing in the Ashmolean Museum (BB. 1713 *verso*), on the front of which are the outlines of part of the interior of San Lorenzo, which can be dated 1532. This leads Tolnay to suppose that Michelangelo may have planned a fresco of the 'Ascension' for the lunette on the entrance wall of the Church of San Lorenzo, above the reliquary balcony.

106-107. DAVID AND GOLIATH. Black chalk, reproduced in the actual size. New York, Pierpont Morgan Library (I, 32D and 32A).

The Morgan Library possesses altogether four such sketches; the two reproduced here are the best.

The sketches are directly developed out of the battle scenes in the Oxford drawing (No. 105). The figure of David looks boyish by the side of the gigantic Goliath.[102]

Formerly in the Reynolds, Breadalbane, Leighton, and Fairfax Murray collections.

108. EXPULSION OF THE MONEY-CHANGERS FROM THE TEMPLE. Black chalk. $5\frac{1}{8} \times 6\frac{1}{4}$ in. London, British Museum (1860-6-16-1).

See text to No. 105.
On the back are some light sketches of figures.

109. EXPULSION OF THE MONEY-CHANGERS FROM THE TEMPLE. Black chalk. $5\frac{1}{2} \times 10\frac{5}{8}$ in. London, British Museum (1860-6-16-2).

See text to No. 105.
On the back are some light sketches of figures and buildings.

110. EXPULSION OF THE MONEY-CHANGERS FROM THE TEMPLE. Black chalk. $6\frac{3}{4} \times 14\frac{1}{2}$ in. London, British Museum (1860-6-16-3).

This sheet, consisting of six pieces of paper pasted together, represents the last version of the theme, more or less as Marcello Venusti used it for his painting of the Expulsion of the Money-changers in the National Gallery, London (No. 1194). See St. Mark, xi, 15.

The three drawings, Nos. 108, 109 and 110, were formerly in the Lawrence and King William II of Holland collections.

111. THREE STUDIES FOR THE PIETÀ AND TWO STUDIES FOR THE ENTOMBMENT. Black chalk. $4\frac{3}{8} \times 11\frac{1}{8}$ in. Oxford, Ashmolean Museum (No. 70).

Two separate sheets, pasted together.

Robinson (32, p. 81 f.) recognized that the two sketches for the Pietà had some connexion with the marble group of the Rondanini Pietà and his dating of it, about 1541, may also be accepted.[103] But the Rondanini Pietà was Michelangelo's last work, and was still unfinished at the time of his death,[104] for which reason Brinckmann dates this drawing in the 1560's,

while Frey, who adheres to the correct dating, about 1541, denies that it is a preliminary study for the Rondanini Pietà.[105] One of Michelangelo's habits as an artist was that he would return time after time to the same motive—especially to body motives. If we keep this fact in mind, the difficulty of judging this drawing disappears. Robinson, Frey and Berenson have dated the drawing correctly, namely, about 1541-42,[106] while the Rondanini Pietà, executed in the main after 1555, as regards the movement motive undoubtedly has a very close connexion with these sketches, though that does not justify the assumption that after so many years Michelangelo made a direct use of this very drawing when he began work on the sculpture. Moreover, both the Pietà sketches and the two for the Entombment have their forerunners among Michelangelo's drawings (and we know how few of these have been preserved), these being three sheets dating from about ten years before the present drawing—the Pietà in Vienna (No. 87), the Entombment in Oxford (No. 88), and two sketches in the upper right corner of the Haarlem Crucifixion (No. 89).[107]

No. 111 was formerly in the Ottley and Lawrence collections.

112. STUDIES FOR A CHRIST ON THE CROSS. Black chalk. $12\frac{1}{2} \times 8\frac{3}{4}$ in. Haarlem, Teyler Museum (No. 22).

This is a sketch for the earliest version of the 'Crucifixion', the original of which has been lost, only two copies, at Windsor Castle (Cat. No. 460) and in the Louvre (Thode, 495), having been preserved. The later version (No. 128) should be compared with it. The present sketch dates from about 1540, or even earlier; the other version was made at least fifteen years later.

With the exception of Thode and Johannes Wilde (41, p. 266), all the more recent critics think that No. 112 is not by Michelangelo. In style it agrees with the sketches for the 'Last Judgement'. (Cf. also Plate 90.)

On the back are some outline sketches.

113. CRUCIFIXION FOR VITTORIA COLONNA. Black chalk. $14\frac{1}{2} \times 10\frac{3}{4}$ in. London, British Museum (1895-9-15-504).

Robinson (32, p. 87) discusses the copy of this drawing in Oxford without mentioning the original. There is another copy in the Louvre. Frey and Berenson believe that the present drawing is only a copy, but Thode maintains that it is the original. In more recent times only Johannes Wilde (41, p. 259) has accepted Thode's opinion. In technique, it is close to the carefully executed drawings of the Cavalieri period (cf. especially No. 92), but the style in this case is more developed, in that the outlines are more sharply stressed and the shadows more subdued. Moreover, No. 113 actually belongs to a later period. Of the copious correspondence between Michelangelo and Vittoria Colonna only seven letters have been preserved, two of these being from Michelangelo; these letters are undated. In the latest letter from Vittoria Colonna to Michelangelo, we read beneath the signature: 'From the convent in Viterbo, on the 20th July.' Vittoria Colonna lived in the convent of Santa Caterina at Viterbo from the autumn of 1541

---

[102] Thode (VI, p. 163) pointed out that Daniele da Volterra used these sketches for his painting of 'David vanquishing Goliath' (Louvre, No. 1462). The engraving by B. Audran (1716) attributes the painting to Michelangelo.

[103] 'Judging from the style of the present sketch it appears to belong to about the time of the completion of the Last Judgement, probably *circa* 1541-42.' For the rest Robinson assumes that the Rondanini Pietà was begun about 1541, before the Pietà in Florence Cathedral, and that the work was then interrupted for a long time and subsequently resumed. One must not forget that, in addition to the Rondanini Pietà, Michelangelo also executed a second, similar group, for it is extremely doubtful whether the Pietà which was in a shop in Rome about 1650 (Thode, V, p. 279), or the Pietà which de Brosses saw in 1739 in the Palazzo Giustiniani, are identical with the Rondanini group.

[104] *The Sculptures of Michelangelo*, 2nd Phaidon edition, 1950, Plate 143. Daniele da Volterra saw Michelangelo working on this Pietà a few days before his death; the date of the other Pietà, the one in Florence Cathedral, is established by a reference in Condivi's biography, written in 1553—in the forty-seventh paragraph he says that Michelangelo has it 'now' in hand.

[105] Charles de Tolnay (*The Rondanini Pietà* in *Burlington Magazine*, Vol. 65, 1934, p. 146 f.) assumes an eclectic attitude, but reaches some interesting conclusions as regards details. He dates the sketch somewhat earlier than Brinckmann.

[106] Judging by the style, I consider this to be the latest possible date.

[107] The fact that these three drawings have been wrongly attributed by Berenson and some other critics to Sebastiano del Piombo does not affect the chronological order in any way.

until the spring of 1544. The letter must be dated 1542, for in July, 1543, the Marchesa was so ill that her life was almost despaired of, and in July, 1544, she was no longer in Viterbo. As the letter mentions the frescoes in the Cappella Paolina, which were begun in 1542, we have a *terminus post quem* for the letter. The other letters were written from Rome, and may be dated between 1539 and 1541.[108]

The above-mentioned correspondence between Michelangelo and Vittoria Colonna includes the following letters:

(1) Letter written by Vittoria Colonna from Rome. She asks Michelangelo to send her the Crucifixion for a short time, even if it is not quite finished.

(2) Letter from Michelangelo to Vittoria Colonna. The Marchesa has returned the Crucifixion to Michelangelo by the hand of Tommaso de' Cavalieri. At the time of writing she was in the convent of San Silvestro al Monte, not far from Michelangelo's house in the Macel dei Corvi at Rome.

(3) Letter from Vittoria Colonna to Michelangelo. The Marchesa has received the finished drawing of the Crucifixion; she would prefer to keep this original rather than exchange it later for a painting made by an assistant; she says that she has examined the drawing with a magnifying glass and with the aid of a mirror, and has been unable to detect any mistakes.[109]

(4) Letter from Michelangelo to Vittoria Colonna. He sends this letter by the hand of his servant Francesco Urbino and acknowledges receipt of a present from Vittoria Colonna.

(5) Letter from Vittoria Colonna to Michelangelo. She mentions a painting of a Christ, and thinks that the angel on the right of the Saviour is finer than the one on the left. Frey relates this part of the letter to the following passage from Condivi's biography: 'He made, at the request of this lady [Vittoria Colonna], a nude Christ taken down from the Cross, who, as a dead body bereft of life, would have fallen at the feet of His most holy mother, had He not been supported in the arms of two little angels. And she, sitting, with a tearful and grievous countenance, at the foot of the Cross, with her arms apart, raises both her hands to heaven with this lament, which may be read, written on the trunk of the cross: "They think not how much blood it costs"—non si pensa quanto sangue costa.' The painting (or cartoon) of this Pietà has been lost. A list of the engravings (dated 1546 and 1547; cf. Plate 138) and painted copies is given by Thode (V, p. 493 f.). Benedetto Varchi, in his funeral oration for Michelangelo, mentions another present which the master made to Vittoria Colonna—'the statue of a nude Christ, similar to the Minerva Christ, but executed in a

different manner'. This cannot have been a sculptured version of the Pietà we are discussing; on the other hand, we must remember a passage in Condivi's biography, where he is describing the Pietà in Florence Cathedral: 'Christ falls lifeless with all his limbs relapsed, but in an attitude very different from that which Michelangelo made for the Marchioness of Pescara, and from that of the Madonna della Febbre' (the Pietà of 1499 in St. Peter's). As it is unlikely that Condivi would have compared two sculptures with one drawing, we may assume that Michelangelo executed the Colonna Pietà also in marble, not necessarily as a relief (though the replica of a relief by the hand of a pupil in the Vatican Library seems to point to this).

Thode assumes (on the basis of a letter written by the Bishop of Fano) that Vittoria Colonna presented the Pietà to Cardinal Pole in 1546.[110] Pole returned to England in 1554, and such Italian works of art as he brought with him were probably installed in Lambeth Palace, but no trace of Michelangelo's Colonna Pietà has ever been found. There is one copy in England, not mentioned by Thode, in the collection of the Earl of Pembroke, at Wilton House. The frame suggests that this copy came from France.

From the text of the letter mentioned it is not quite clear, however, whether the Marchesa di Pescara was asking for a second version or whether it was already in her possession. The text is reproduced in a study of Vittoria Colonna by Prof. A. Luzio (in *Rivista Stor. Mant.*, I, p. 51 f.) and by Karl Frey (*Michelagniolo Buonarroti, Quellen und Forschungen*, I, 1907, p. 139). In translation the text runs as follows:

'The Bishop of Fano to the Cardinal Ercole Gonzaga.
Trento, May 12, 1546.
'My lord Pole, having heard that your lordship desired a Christ by Michelangelo's hand, charged me to find out secretly if such was the case, because he happens to have one from that master which he would willingly send you; but it is in the shape of a Pietà, although the whole figure is seen. He says it will be no deprivation to him, because he can get another from the Marchesa di Pescara. Will your lordship write to me about it?'

Thus the document itself does not state whether it was a cartoon, a drawing, a painting or a relief, or whether two versions were available; or, lastly, which of the three persons remained in possession of the original—Vittoria Colonna, Cardinal Pole, or Cardinal Ercole Gonzaga.

Michelangelo's acquaintance with Pole is important because it enables us to interpret the deeper meaning of the Pietà (and of drawing No. 113). Pole had quarrelled with his sovereign, Henry VIII of England, over religious matters, and the King, who had not spared More and Fisher, made repeated attempts to have him eliminated by hired assassins. The family of Pole had to atone instead; his brother and cousin were executed for high treason, and on May 27, 1541, his mother, who was seventy-six years old, was beheaded in the Tower by order of the King. Thus the inscription on the Pietà—'They think not how much blood it costs'—acquires a

---

[108] We have proof that Vittoria Colonna was in Rome from March, 1539, to March, 1541 (Frey, 48, pp. 529–530, Itinerary of Vittoria Colonna; cf. *Carteggio di Vittoria Colonna*, ed. E. Ferrero and G. Müller, Turin, 1889). In June, 1544, she was again in Rome, where she died on February 25, 1547, in the convent of Sant'Anna dei Funari.

[109] What she means by 'with the aid of a mirror' is not quite certain. Painters often use mirrors to detect errors of draughtsmanship, which show up more clearly when the picture is inverted. Apart from that, mirrors are used only in order to obtain a concentration of light. I would remind the reader of the following passage in the ninth chapter of Adalbert Stifter's *Nachsommer*: 'I fetched a magnifying glass and with the aid of a mirror we directed a shimmering light on to the spot; I looked at it through the glass and saw the fine crystals of the white marble sparkling before my eyes.'

[110] Thode, V, p. 494; Frey, *Quellen und Forschungen*, p. 139; M. Haile, *Life of Pole*, 1910, p. 323.

new significance. The words are taken from Dante;[111] the lines which follow them have an obvious relationship to the ideas of the 'Spirituali' (to whom Pole, Vittoria Colonna, Contarini, Bishop Giberti, and others belonged), and to their efforts to restore the purity of the Church. 'I see thy little bark, O Peter, so laden with mire that it is in peril of sinking before the first onset of the waves', are the opening words of one of the Marchesa's sonnets.

In 1542, the year in which the Pietà was probably created, Cardinal Pole was residing in Viterbo as papal governor of the city; Vittoria Colonna was in a convent there, and around these two a group of adherents professing the same ideas soon gathered. Spiritually Michelangelo was a member of this group.

The Colonna Crucifixion, although drawn about 1540 and thus somewhat earlier than the Pietà, is animated by the same ideas. Here 'Justification through faith in the completeness of Christ's sacrifice on the Cross' is represented, in accordance with the formula evolved by Pole's friend, Cardinal Contarini, in April, 1541, but known to the circle of the 'Spirituali' long before. In the *Beneficio di Cristo Crocifisso* (which was printed for the first time in 1542 and soon afterwards placed on the Index) we read that we shall find forgiveness for our sins so long as we faithfully cherish the sacrifice of Christ in our souls, and that only through His sinlessness can we find forgiveness for our own sins. Justification through faith 'is a work of God in us by which our old man is crucified and we become a new creature'.

The interpretation we have endeavoured to give brings us to the conclusion that the Colonna Crucifixion is not merely a representation of the Crucified Christ—slightly differentiated in that Christ is here shown with open eyes, alive, as the victory of life over death—but that it was conceived in the atmosphere of a particular religious idea and therefore has a very definite meaning. Michelangelo himself has spoken in similar terms in his poems: 'O flesh, O blood, O Cross, O agony of death, justify me and atone for my sin, in which I, like my father, was born'; or 'Dismayed, bewildered, within me my soul fears for its salvation. O Lord, in my last hour stretch out Thy merciful arms, take me out of myself and make me pleasing to Thee'; or again, 'All my travail is vain, if Thy blood help not mankind. Have mercy upon me, for I was born Thy bondsman'; and lastly: 'The soul cannot find peace in painting or sculpture; it seeks nought but the love of God, which opens its arms towards us from the Cross.'

(6) Letter from Vittoria Colonna to Michelangelo, dated July 20 (1542), from Viterbo. Vittoria asks Michelangelo to write less frequently, otherwise she will neglect her religious exercises and he his painting in the Cappella Paolina. She mentions a drawing (or perhaps a painting) which she has received from Michelangelo—'The Woman of Samaria at the Well'. The original of this, too, has been lost. There is a list of engravings made from it (Plate 139), and of copies in Thode (V, p. 464). The woman of Samaria who gave Jesus water to drink (St. John iv. 7–9) although she knew that He belonged to a people who had no dealings with the Samaritans, symbolizes 'good works'. This reminds us of the advice given to Vittoria Colonna by Cardinal Pole, that she should order her life as if she could only be saved through deeds of mercy, but that she should think as if she could only be saved through faith.[112] Thus interpreted, 'The Woman of Samaria at the Well' is a counterpart to the 'Crucifixion'. There is, however, also a mystical interpretation possible, which would make 'The Woman of Samaria' a counterpart to the 'Pietà'. Both compositions symbolize everlasting life: the one as 'the living water', the other as 'the sacred blood' (St. John iv. 13–14, and vi. 55).

(7) Letter from Vittoria Colonna to Michelangelo, undated, from Rome. Contains only a very general, appreciative mention of Michelangelo's sculptures.

Of the four works which Michelangelo executed for Vittoria Colonna—the Crucifixion, the Pietà,[113] the 'Woman of Samaria at the Well', and the marble statue of Christ—the only one that has been preserved is the drawing we are discussing.

Formerly in the collections of the King of Naples, Brunet, Lawrence, King William II of Holland, Brooks (Liverpool), Malcolm.

114. LAMENTATION FOR CHRIST. Black chalk. $11 \times 10\frac{5}{8}$ in. London, British Museum (1896–7–10–1).

This celebrated Pietà came from the Warwick collection. It was attributed by Berenson (1903 and 1938), d'Achiardi (1908) and Pallucchini (1944) to Sebastiano del Piombo, and by E. Panofsky (in *Festschrift für J. Schlosser*, 1927) to Daniele da Volterra. Thode (V, p. 496 f.) rightly adheres to the attribution to Michelangelo, which has recently been defended again by Johannes Wilde (41, p. 257). There is a study for the figure of St. John, on the extreme right, at Windsor Castle (Cat. No. 433).

The drawing has a stylistic relationship to the four following plates (Nos. 115–118), for which reason I date it from the time when Michelangelo started work on the frescoes in the Cappella Paolina, i.e. about 1542. It is not impossible that this drawing and the study in Windsor were intended for a painting subsequently executed by Sebastiano del Piombo, by Venusti, or by Daniele da Volterra, but on the other hand it is equally possible that Michelangelo with these drawings was preparing to make a presentation drawing for Vittoria Colonna.

On the back of the sheet is a study in red chalk, presumably for a Flagellation; not by Michelangelo.

115. THE VIRGIN BENEATH THE CROSS. Black chalk. 9×4 in. Paris, Louvre (No. 720 *recto*).

This study and the following one were intended for the

---

[111] *Paradiso*, XXIX, 91 (Thode, V, p. 494 f.). 'They think not how great the cost of blood to sow the scripture in the world, and how he pleases who humbly keeps by its side. Each one strains his wit to make a show and plies his inventions; and these are handled by the preachers and the Gospel left in silence. . . . Fables are proclaimed from the pulpit on this side and on that . . . Christ said not to his first assembly: "Go and preach trifles in the world", but gave to them the true foundation; that, and that only, sounded on their lips. . . . Now they go forth with jests and with grimaces to preach, and if loud laughter rise, the hood inflates and no more is required. But such a bird is nesting in the hood-tail that if the crowd should see it, they would see what indulgence they are trusting in.'

[112] *Estratto del Processo di Pietro Carnesecchi*, ed. G. Manzoni, in *Miscellanea di Storia Italiana*, Vol. X, 1870, p. 269.

[113] The Berlin Museum possesses a relief replica of the Crucifixion (Cat. 1933, No. 327), and also a relief in red wax of a Pietà (Cat. No. 268), different from the relief in the Vatican.

elaborated version of the Colonna Crucifixion (No. 113), of which Venusti made a painted copy for Tommaso de' Cavalieri (Thode, V, p. 469). A copy of this kind by Venusti is now in the Galleria Borghese, Rome (No. 422), and there is another in the Uffizi (Plate 137).

The figure has resemblances to the 'Woman of Samaria' (which was discussed above under No. 113; cf. Plate 139), mentioned in a letter from Vittoria Colonna written in 1542, which is also the date of the present and the following drawing.

Much cut on all four sides.

Formerly in the Coypel collection.

No. 120 is on the back of the sheet.

116. ST. JOHN BENEATH THE CROSS. Black chalk. $9\frac{3}{4} \times 3\frac{1}{4}$ in. Paris, Louvre (No. 698).

See the text to No. 115.

Formerly in the Jabach and Coypel collections.

117. FRAGMENT OF A CARTOON FOR THE 'CRUCIFIXION OF ST. PETER'. Charcoal drawing. $103\frac{1}{2} \times 61\frac{1}{2}$ in. Naples, Museo Nazionale (No. 398).

The cartoon shows the figures in the left bottom corner of the fresco of the 'Crucifixion of St. Peter' in the Cappella Paolina in Rome, which was begun in 1542. The outlines are pricked for transfer. This is the only cartoon preserved for a fresco by Michelangelo and Berenson's vaguely indicated doubts as to its authenticity are not, in my opinion, justified. On the other hand, it is true that the cartoon has been repaired and, in parts, much restored, but whether this restoration was done by Daniele da Volterra, is impossible to say.

(See E. Steinmann, *Cartoni di Michelangelo*, in *Bollettino d'Arte*, ser. 2a, *anno* V, 1925–26, p. 3 f.)

118. CARTOON OF A HOLY FAMILY. Charcoal drawing on brown paper. $92 \times 73\frac{1}{2}$ in. London, British Museum (Malcolm Collection, No. 81).

Vasari says of Condivi: 'He spent several years over a picture for which Michelangelo had given him the cartoon, and, at a word, the hopes he conceived of him, vanished in smoke. I remember that Michelangelo, having compassion on Condivi's hard labours, would sometimes help him with his own hands, but it was all to little purpose.' Vasari is probably referring to his stay in Rome from 1542 to 1544; only at that time did Vasari become better acquainted with Michelangelo, and was even permitted to live for some time in the Master's house in Rome (W. Kallab, *Vasaristudien*, 1908, pp. 72–73). Leoni, who, on behalf of Michelangelo's family, dealt with the Master's estate, describes one of the four cartoons Michelangelo left as being that 'from which Ascanio Condivi painted'. Daniele da Volterra, in a letter dated March 17, 1564, calls the cartoon an 'Epiphany' and mentions Condivi's painted copy (now in the Casa Buonarroti; Thode, III, p. 703). The cartoon, handed over to the notary who wound up the estate, was later in the Casa Buonarroti and in the Wicar, Lawrence, Woodburn and Malcolm collections. The pedigree of the cartoon is thus well documented, and in its style there is nothing to make one doubt Michelangelo's authorship. The St. John (on the left) is reminiscent of the Adam in the 'Last Judgement'; the legs of the Virgin resemble those of the Christ judging. Nevertheless, there are still stronger resemblances to figures in the Paolina chapel frescoes. As the 'Last Judgement' was finished in 1541

and the Paolina frescoes were begun in 1542, we can, if we also take into account the passage from Vasari quoted above, date the cartoon about 1542.

The cartoon is in a bad state of preservation and has been restored in places.

119. CHRIST TAKING LEAVE OF HIS MOTHER. Black chalk. $10\frac{5}{8} \times 6\frac{1}{4}$ in. Cambridge, Fitzwilliam Museum (Clough Collection, No. 23).

Front and back of a sheet. The cartoon for which these studies were made formed part of Michelangelo's estate, and was handed over to Tommaso de' Cavalieri (Gotti, II, p. 155; Thode, V, p. 502); the cartoon, which has since been lost, is also mentioned in a letter from Daniele da Volterra to Vasari dated March 7, 1564 (Gotti, I, p. 357).

The figure on the back (No. 119A) shows some relationship to the Adam in the 'Expulsion from the Garden of Eden' on the Sistine Chapel ceiling, to the sketch for the 'Noli me tangere' (No. 70) and, above all, to the St. John of the 'Epiphany' (No. 118). The drawing on the front (No. 119B) is reminiscent in its technique of the London Annunciation (No. 126); in its movement, of the Christ in the 'Woman of Samaria at the Well', which dates from 1542 (Plate 139), and also of the Christ in the 'Expulsion of the Money-changers' (No. 110), drawn about 1541 for Venusti. It is very possible that the cartoon of the 'Christ taking leave of His Mother' was originally intended for a painting to be executed by Venusti. On the basis of these comparisons with compositions dating from about 1542, we can date the present drawing shortly after that year.

120. SKETCH FOR A FIGURE BENEATH THE CROSS. Black chalk. 9×4 in. Paris, Louvre (No. 720 *verso*).

On the front of this sheet is the finished drawing of a Virgin beneath the Cross (No. 115), which I have dated about 1542, and the same date is also applicable to the sketch on the back. According to Thode, it is only a light preliminary drawing for the figure on the other side of the sheet, viz., the Virgin; this would show that Michelangelo used a male model even for the Mother of God. I believe, however, that he was thinking of another version of the Crucifixion, rather in the style of No. 125. The sheet has been badly cut, especially on the right.

121. SKETCH FOR A MAN STRIDING FORWARDS. Black chalk. $8\frac{1}{8} \times 4\frac{7}{8}$ in. Oxford, Ashmolean Museum (No. 60).

The figure has resemblance to that of the man supporting the right arm of Christ in the third and fourth sketches on No. 111, and also to the man carrying a lance in the 'Crucifixion of St. Peter' in the Cappella Paolina. This fresco was begun in 1542, and the present drawing cannot be much later. The angel supporting the right arm of Christ in the Colonna Pietà (see Plate 138) corresponds best with the figure of No. 121. (Compare also Berenson, Fig. 716.) This connexion also leads to a dating about 1542.

On the back of the sheet is a female figure in an attitude of yearning.

Formerly in the Casa Buonarroti and the Wicar and Lawrence collections.

122. VIRGIN OF THE ANNUNCIATION. Black chalk. $14 \times 8\frac{7}{8}$ in. London, British Museum (1900–6–11–1).

D'Achiardi (*Sebastiano del Piombo*, 1908, p. 319) attributed this drawing to Sebastiano del Piombo because of an alleged relationship to the Warwick Pietà (No. 114). In the movement it has a still more marked resemblance to the St. John the Evangelist in the 'Epiphany' (No. 118) and, from the purely technical point of view, to Nos. 125 and 127. No other critic agrees with this incomprehensible attribution by d'Achiardi. Frey expressed doubts as to the authenticity of the drawing (and was not quite certain about the related drawing, No. 126). Vasari (VII, p. 575) says: 'From designs and works of Michelangelo, Marcello [Venusti] has made numerous little pictures. . . . Nay, of truth, for small things it would not be easy to find better pictures; wherefore that kindly gentleman Tommaso de' Cavalieri, who has always favoured Marcello, employed him to paint for the church of San Giovanni in Laterano an Annunciation, after the design of Michelangelo. . . . The cartoon, by Michelangelo's own hand, was presented to Duke Cosimo by Leonardo Buonarroti, nephew of Michelangelo, together with other designs.'

The cartoon has been lost; the present drawing, one of Michelangelo's finest, may be held to be a preliminary study for the cartoon (cf. also Plate 142).

In the treatment of the folds, in the proportions and, in part, in the movement, the drawing is reminiscent of the 'Rachel' on the tomb of Pope Julius; this statue was executed between 1542 and 1545, and the drawing must be dated from the same period.

123. APOSTLE WITH A BOOK. Black chalk. 7 × 5¼ in. Haarlem, Teyler Museum (No. 18).

Our reproduction shows only a part of the drawing.

The sheet also contains a sketch, on the left edge, of the upper part of the same figure's body; below, upside down, are two faint sketches of figures hastening forward; in addition, there is a sketch of a building, which Marcuard, Thode and Berenson think has some connexion with the work on the dome of St. Peter's. According to the same critics, the present figure sketch (and other similar sketches; Thode, V, p. 168) was intended for the decorations on the inside of the dome. If this supposition is correct, the sheet could be dated about 1546–47, when Michelangelo prepared the first model and was appointed chief architect. In any case, such a dating is stylistically justified.

The figure has a certain resemblance to Sebastiano del Piombo's fresco of 'St. Peter' in the church of San Pietro in Montorio in Rome; rather surprisingly, although it has considerable affinity to No. 122, this drawing has never been attributed to Sebastiano. On the other hand, an attempt, supported by very skilful arguments,[114] has been made to attribute it to Daniele da Volterra, with reference to the fact that the drawing on the back of the sheet (Plate 190) was used by Daniele da Volterra in his painting of 'Mercury ordering Aeneas to abandon Dido'. Berenson admits this, but still adheres to the attribution of the drawing to Michelangelo, on which point I agree with him. In this sense, the present sketch does not differ in any respect from the drawings Michelangelo made for Sebastiano del Piombo, Marcello Venusti and others.

124. ANGEL. Black chalk. 7½ × 11 in. London, British Museum (1895-9-15-516 verso).

Indistinct sketch of a Pietà, partly resembling the Colonna Pietà and partly the Pietà in Florence Cathedral, which points to a date between 1542 and 1548.[115] Over this barely recognizable sketch has an angel hastening forward been drawn.

No. 126 is on the back of the sheet.

Formerly in the Casa Buonarroti and the Wicar, Lawrence and Malcolm collections.

125. CHRIST ON THE CROSS. Black chalk. 8½ × 7⅞ in. Oxford, Ashmolean Museum (No. 72).

This drawing seems to me to be much earlier than the late versions of the Crucifixion in Paris, Windsor and London; it has been developed out of the second version of the Colonna Crucifixion (Plate 137). A point that worried Thode is the fact that, contrary to tradition, a male figure is shown on the right and a female (?) figure on the left of the Cross. I believe that the figure on the left is St. Peter,[116] denying Christ as he hastens away, and that the figure on the right is St. John, standing weeping beneath the Cross. The short girdled coat of the St. John is also found in a Crucifixion at Windsor (Fig. 14 on p. 58). Both figures are reminiscent in their proportions of the personages in the top and bottom right corners of the 'Crucifixion of St. Peter', and also of figures in the other fresco in the Cappella Paolina, the 'Conversion of St. Paul'. The first fresco was finished about 1546 and the second was begun about that time; this date seems to me to be applicable to the present drawing.

Formerly in the Casa Buonarroti and the Wicar and Lawrence collections.

126. THE ANNUNCIATION. Black chalk. 11 × 7½ in. London, British Museum (1895-9-15-516 recto).

Despite the fact that the forms are not completely dissolved, this is a relatively late drawing. The treatment of the draperies is reminiscent of the Florentine Pietà. The present drawing dates from about 1550. Attributed to Daniele da Volterra by F. Baumgart (Bollettino d'Arte, XXVIII, 1934, p. 346–347). No. 124 is on the back of the sheet.

127. THE ANNUNCIATION. Black chalk. 8½ × 7½ in. Oxford, Ashmolean Museum (No. 74).

The note in the upper left corner, transcribed by Thode and containing the words 'Pasquino' and 'Casteldurante', provides a terminus post quem for this drawing. From 1556 on the widow of Michelangelo's servant Urbino lived in Casteldurante and Michelangelo used to send her messages by the hand of Pasquino. The correspondence between Michelangelo and the widow lasted until 1561, and was particularly frequent about 1559 (cf. Frey, Sammlung ausgewählter Briefe an Michelagniolo Buonarroti, 1899, No. 351 f.).

The angel is of huge dimensions and is hovering just above the ground, as if he had tried to alight but was unable to do so—a pentimento of a right leg resting on the ground is visible. The visionary spirit of this drawing and the complete dissolution of the forms are reminiscent of the Rondanini Pietà, on which Michelangelo was working at the same time.

For purposes of comparison No. 126 and No. 127, since they are the two late versions of the theme, are reproduced on opposite pages; nevertheless I think there is an interval of several years between the two.

Formerly in the Casa Buonarroti and the Wicar and Lawrence collections.

---

[114] Johannes Wilde, in Belvedere, 1927, p. 142 f.
[115] The Florentine Pietà is already mentioned in the first edition of Vasari, published in 1550.

[116] Left, as seen by the spectator, i.e. the figure on the right of the Cross. As regards the type, cf. No. 123, which in all probability also represents St. Peter.

FIG. 13.—Crucifixion. Louvre (BB. 1583).

FIG. 14.—Crucifixion. Windsor (BB. 1622).

128. CHRIST ON THE CROSS BETWEEN THE VIRGIN AND ST. JOHN. Black chalk. 15¾ × 8⅝ in. Windsor Castle, Royal Library (Inv. No. 12761).

For the St. John a drawing made at the time of the painted version of the Colonna Crucifixion (cf. Plates 116 and 137) was used, but the present drawing dates from a later period and is not much earlier than No. 127, i.e. about 1556.

According to Brinckmann the chronology of the Crucifixions of the late period is as follows: (1) The present drawing; (2) Windsor Castle, Cat. No. 436, Fig. 14; (3) Louvre, Thode 471, Berenson 1583, Fig. 13; (4) British Museum, Thode 357, Berenson 1530, our No. 129. The other version in the British Museum, Thode 356, Berenson 1529, our No. 131, is evidently, in the opinion of Brinckmann, who does not mention it, only a variant of (1). In this connexion he remarks: 'Concerning the chronology of the present drawings, there will doubtless be much discussion, which in the main will lead to no results.' (Cf. R. Wittkower, in *Burlington Magazine*, Vol. LXXVIII, 1941, p. 159 f.). On the back of No. 128 is a leg study in black chalk.

129. CHRIST ON THE CROSS BETWEEN THE VIRGIN AND ST. JOHN. Black chalk. 16⅛ × 11¼ in. London, British Museum (1895-9-15-510).

See the text to No. 128. Numerous *pentimenti* and light retouchings in white.

Formerly in the Casa Buonarroti and the Wicar, Lawrence and Malcolm collections.

130. VIRGIN AND CHILD. Black chalk. 10½ × 4¾ in. London, British Museum (1859-6-25-562).

The figure is, as Thode pointed out, derived from the Virgin in No. 129. Thode assigns the same date to both drawings. I do not know of any drawings later than the present one, and would date it rather later than No. 127, i.e. about 1560.

Formerly in the Casa Buonarroti.

131. CHRIST ON THE CROSS BETWEEN THE VIRGIN AND ST. JOHN. Black chalk. 16⅛ × 11¼ in. London, British Museum (1895-9-15-509).

Reproduced as coloured frontispiece.

See the text to No. 128.

Both the flanking figures reveal numerous *pentimenti* and vigorous retouching in white.

No. 131 is closest to the version in the Louvre (reproduced here as Fig. 13), but in No. 131 the Cross is Y-shaped. I believe the present drawing to be somewhat later than No. 128. The drawing was previously in the same collections as No. 129.

THE PLATES

AN ASTERISK (*) IN FRONT OF THE NUMBER INDICATES THAT THE
REPRODUCTION IS IN THE SAME SIZE AS THE ORIGINAL
(ALSO PLATES 37, 62, 69, 115)

CORRECTIONS TO THE CAPTIONS

9. Vienna (not Munich). 37. Delete *College*. 62. Two Figures struggling. 193. *Read*: black chalk drawing (not pen and ink).

The descriptive titles of the drawings and the names of the collections are given in abbreviated form in the captions
For fuller descriptions see the corresponding numbers in the Catalogue.

1. COPY OF FIGURES FROM A FRESCO BY GIOTTO · ABOUT 1489 · LOUVRE

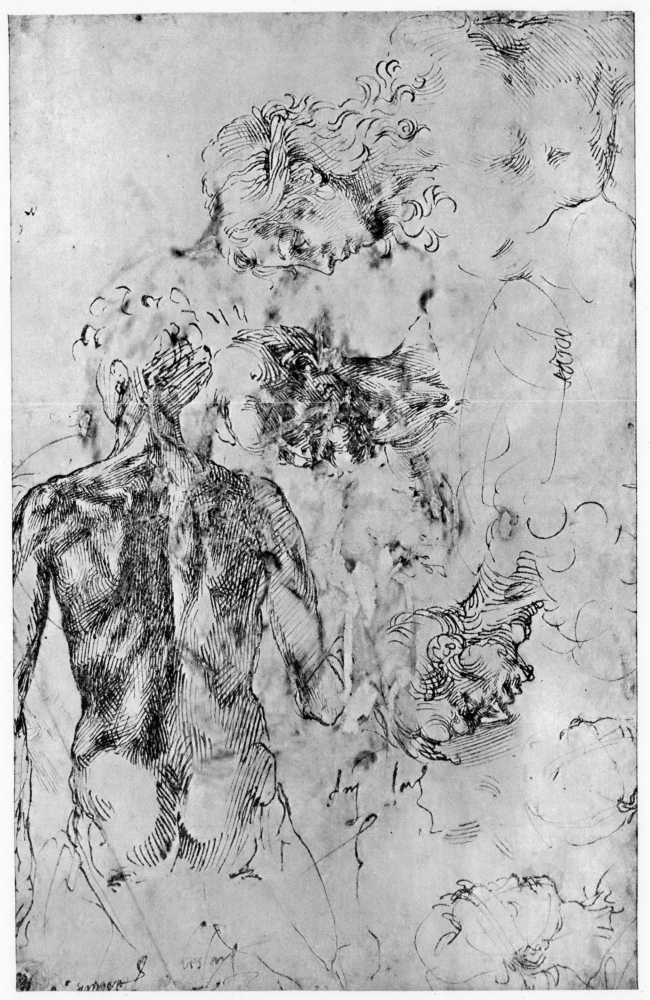

*7. STUDY OF A NUDE TORSO AND VARIOUS HEADS · ABOUT 1501 · OXFORD

*8. ST. ANNE, THE VIRGIN AND THE INFANT CHRIST · ABOUT 1501 · OXFORD

*9. SKETCH FOR THE BRONZE DAVID AND STUDY OF A RIGHT ARM · 1501–02 · LOUVRE

10. STUDIES FROM ANTIQUE SCULPTURES · ABOUT 1501 · LOUVRE

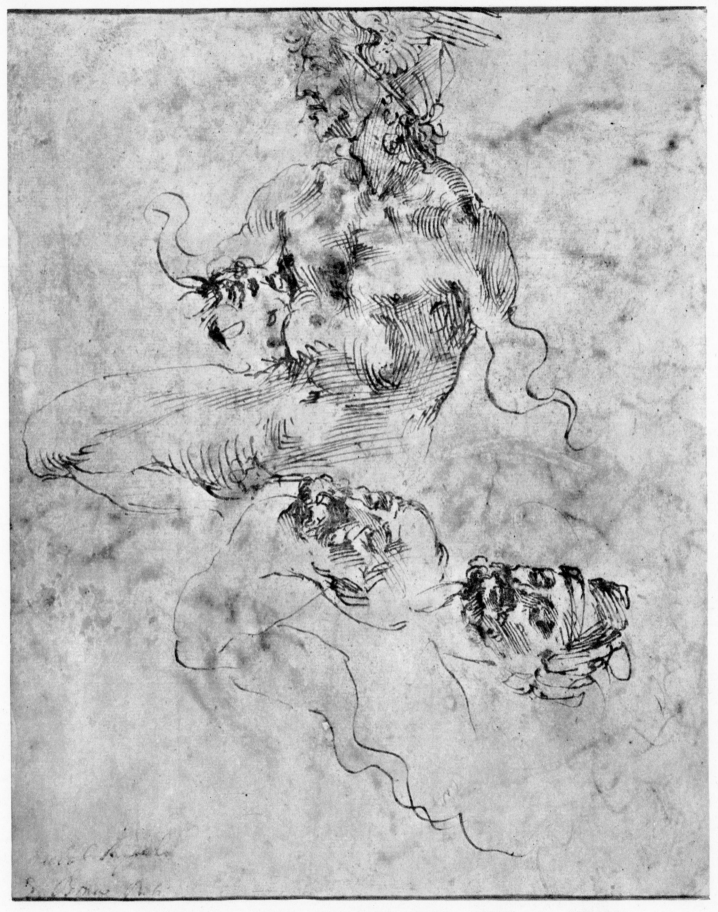

*11. STUDIES FOR A TRITON AND THREE HEADS · ABOUT 1501 · OXFORD

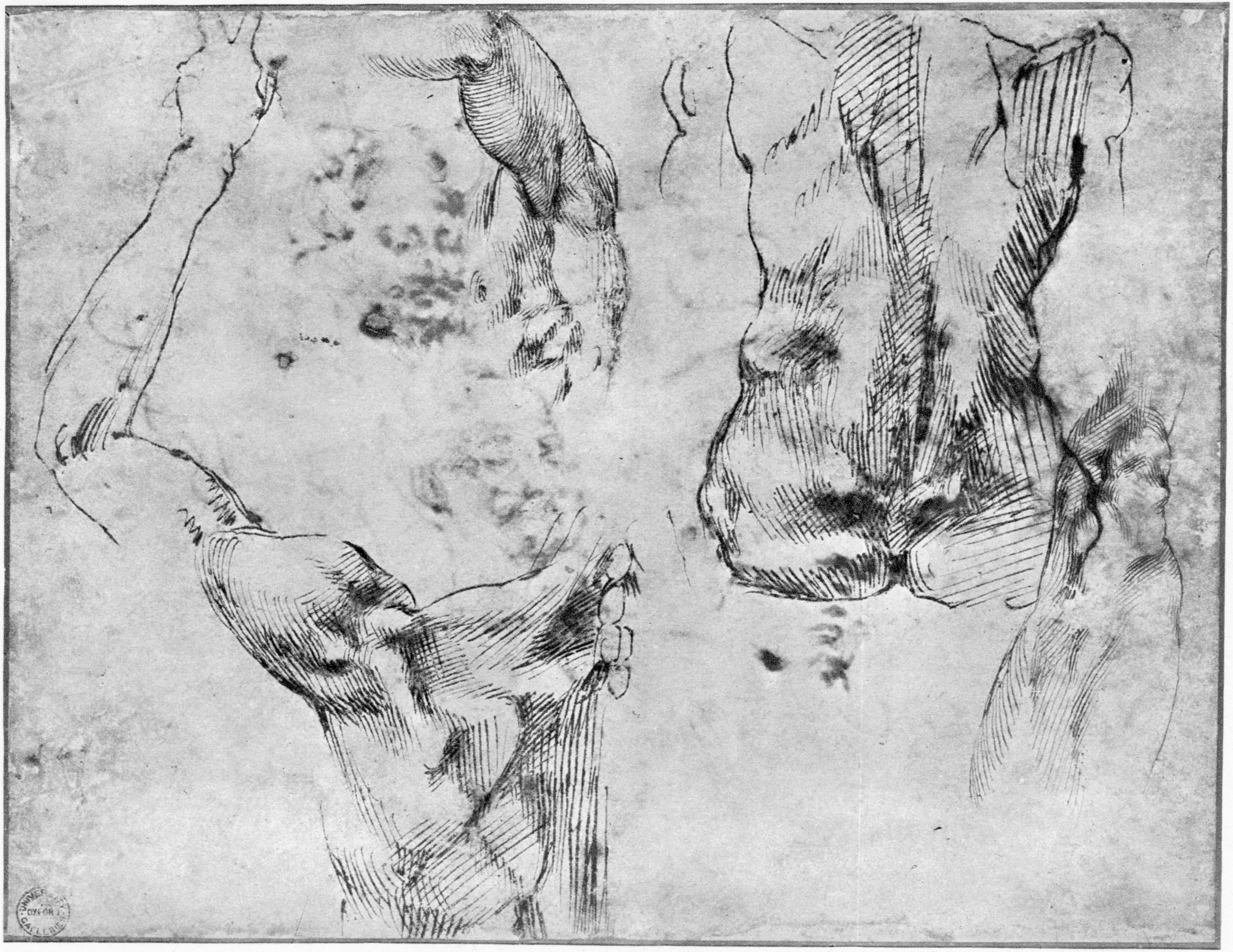

*12. STUDIES FROM THE NUDE . ABOUT 1501 · OXFORD

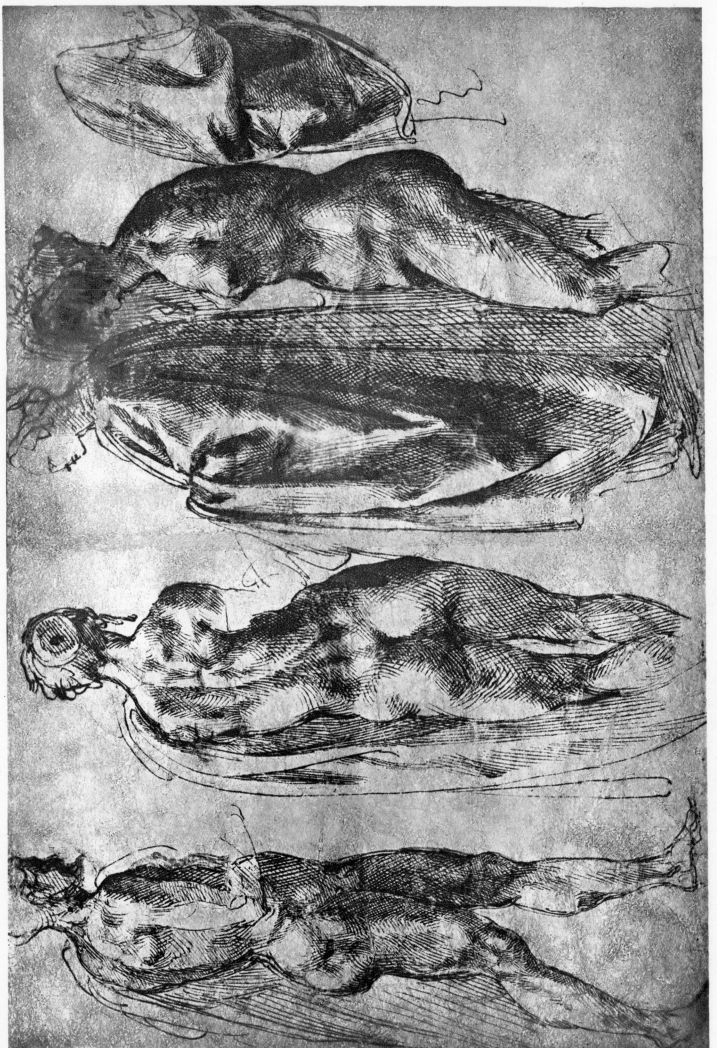

14. STUDY FOR ONE OF THE THREE MAGI · ABOUT 1503 · BRITISH MUSEUM

*15. FAUN · ABOUT 1503 · BRITISH MUSEUM

16. YOUTH WITH LEFT ARM EXTENDED · ABOUT 1504 · BRITISH MUSEUM

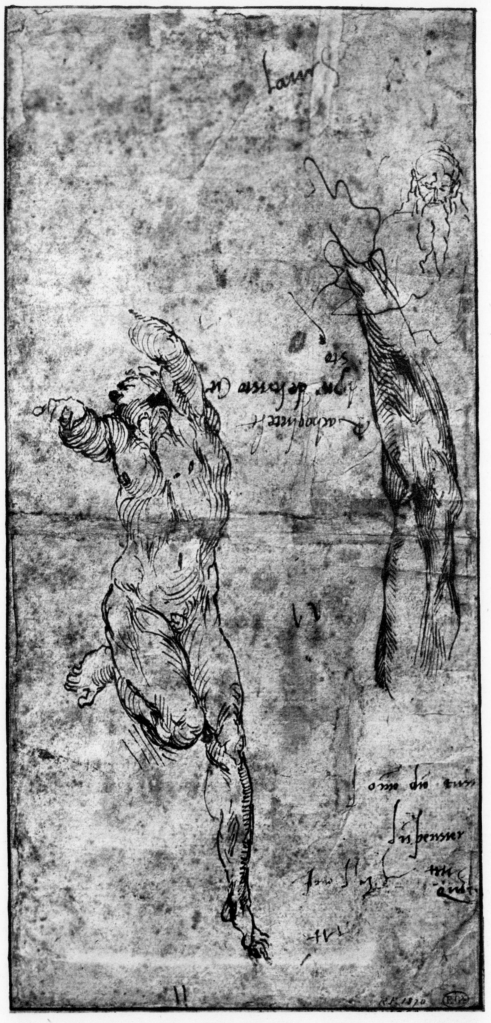

17. NUDE YOUTH AND OTHER STUDIES · ABOUT 1504 · LOUVRE

*18. NUDE SEEN FROM THE BACK · ABOUT 1504 · CASA BUONARROTI

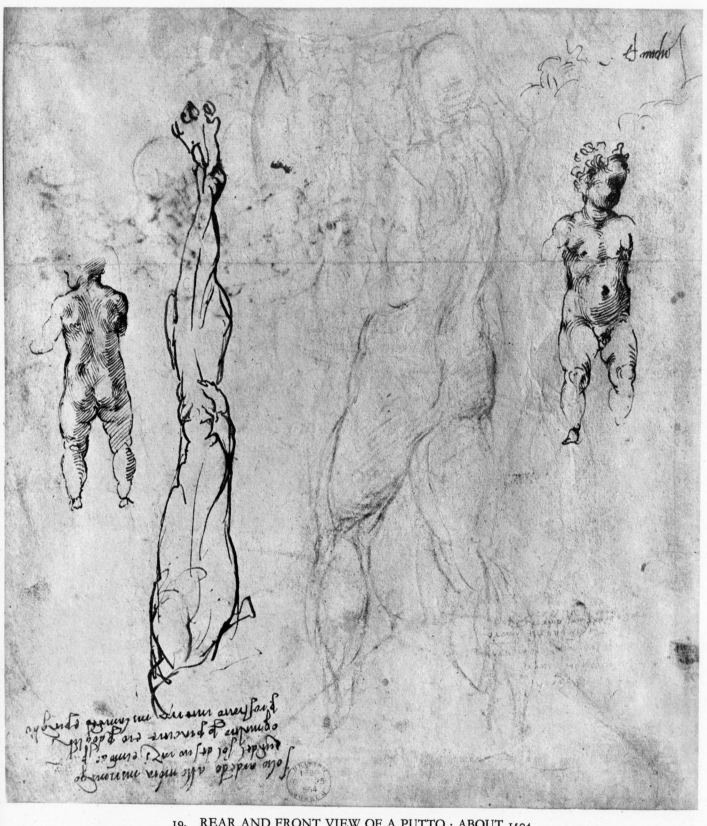

19. REAR AND FRONT VIEW OF A PUTTO · ABOUT 1504
NUDE SEEN FROM THE BACK; STUDY OF A LEFT LEG AND VERSES OF A LATER DATE
BRITISH MUSEUM

27. HEAD STUDY FOR THE SISTINE CEILING · ABOUT 1509 · LOUVRE

le fezze me tane

28. STUDY OF A PROFILE · 1509–13 · UFFIZI

*29. HEAD STUDY FOR THE PROPHET JONAH · ABOUT 1511 · CASA BUONARROTI

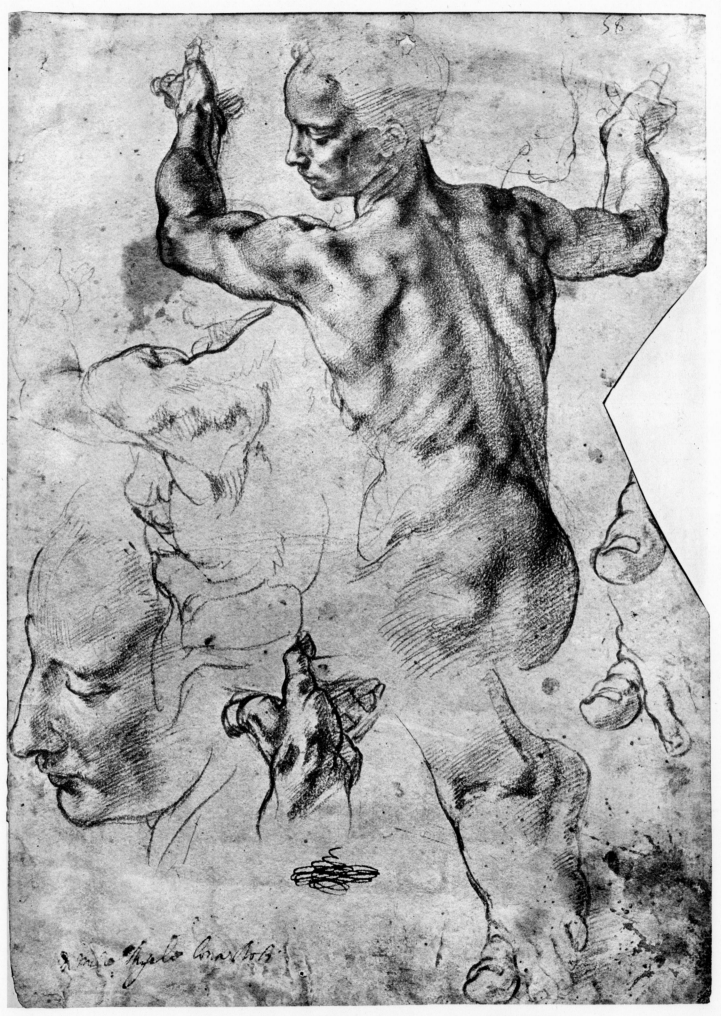

30. STUDIES FOR THE LIBYAN SIBYL · 1511–12 · NEW YORK

31. JUDITH WITH THE HEAD OF HOLOFERNES · 1512-13 · LOUVRE

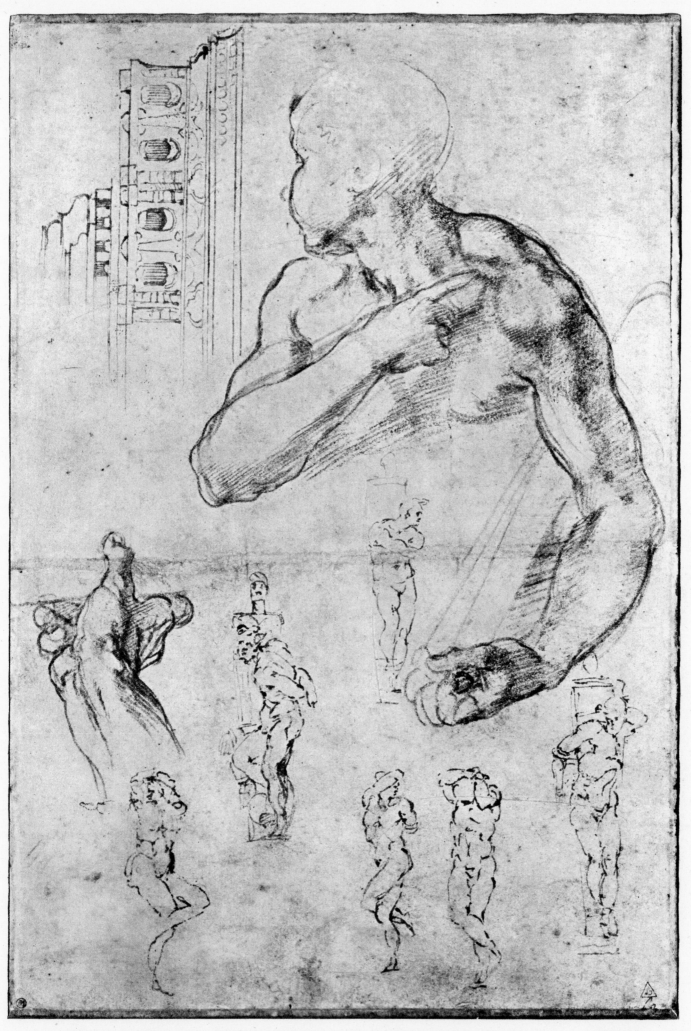

32. SKETCHES FOR THE SISTINE CEILING AND THE TOMB OF JULIUS · 1512–13 · OXFORD

33. SEATED FIGURE AND PUTTO FOR THE TOMB OF JULIUS · 1512–13 · BRITISH MUSEUM

34. SIBYL AND PUTTO FOR THE TOMB OF JULIUS · 1513 · LOUVRE

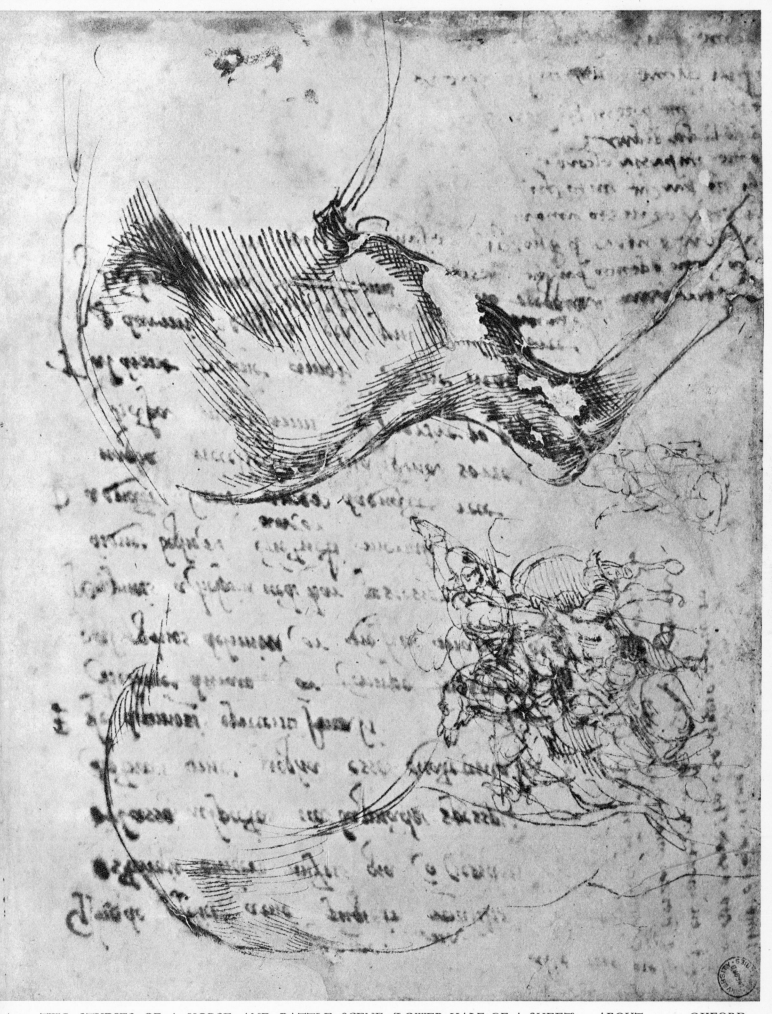

*45. TWO STUDIES OF A HORSE, AND BATTLE SCENE (LOWER HALF OF A SHEET) · ABOUT 1520 · OXFORD

Michel Angelo Buonarota

*46. COMBAT OF CAVALRY AND FOOT SOLDIERS · ABOUT 1520 · OXFORD

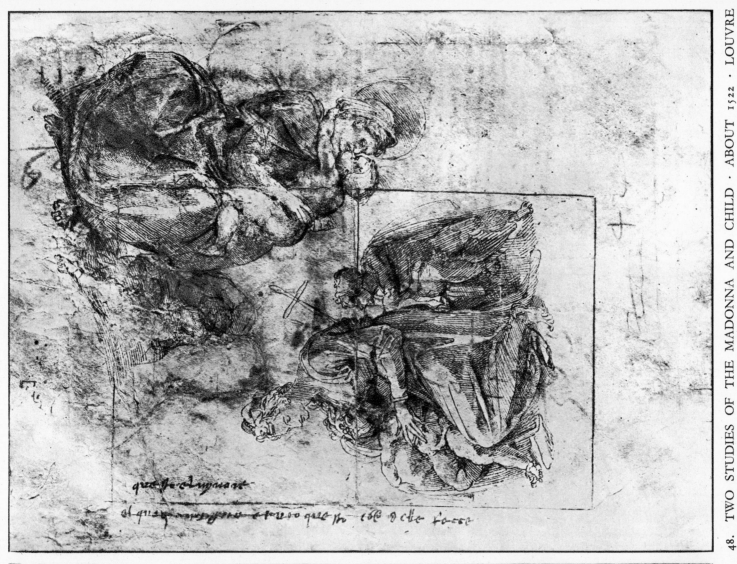

48. TWO STUDIES OF THE MADONNA AND CHILD · ABOUT 1522 · LOUVRE

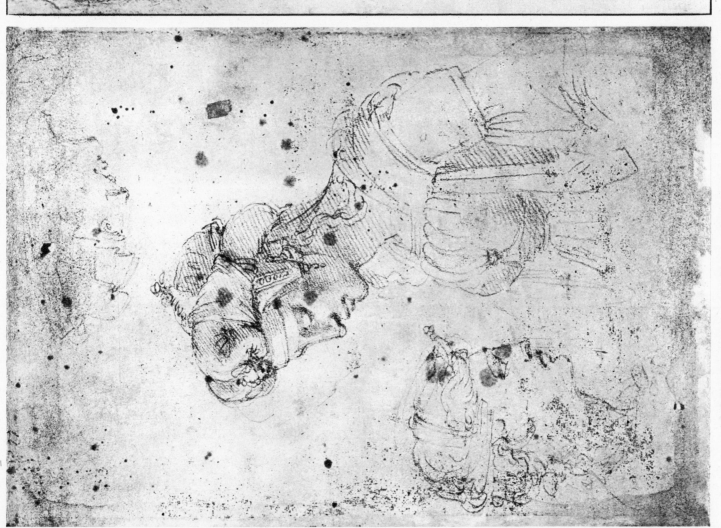

47. THREE FEMALE HEADS · ABOUT 1522 · UFFIZI

49. 'DAMNED SOUL' · ABOUT 1522 · UFFIZI

50. VENUS, MARS AND CUPID · ABOUT 1522 · UFFIZI

51. THREE FEMALE PROFILES · ABOUT 1522 · UFFIZI

52. GIRL HOLDING A DISTAFF · ABOUT 1524 · BRITISH MUSEUM

53. TWO SKETCHES OF THE MADONNA AND CHILD · 1524 · BRITISH MUSEUM

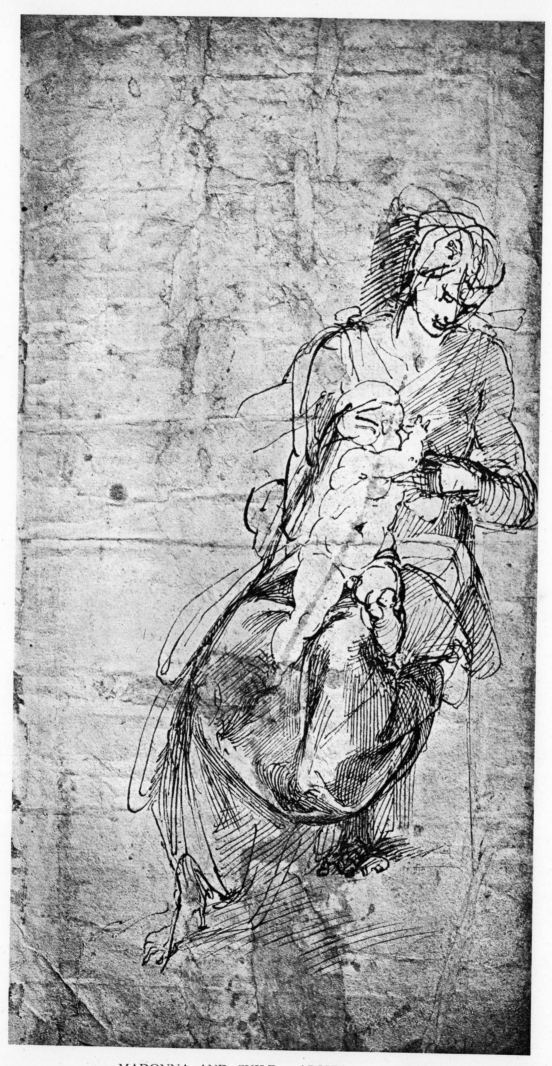

54. MADONNA AND CHILD · ABOUT 1524 · VIENNA

62. TWO WRESTLERS · ABOUT 1530 · HAARLEM   63. DECORATIVE MASK · ABOUT 1530 · WINDSOR

64. DESIGN FOR SMALL PLASTIC WORKS · ABOUT 1530 · FOGG MUSEUM OF ART

*65. PROFILE WITH FANTASTIC HEAD-DRESS · ABOUT 1528-30 · OXFORD

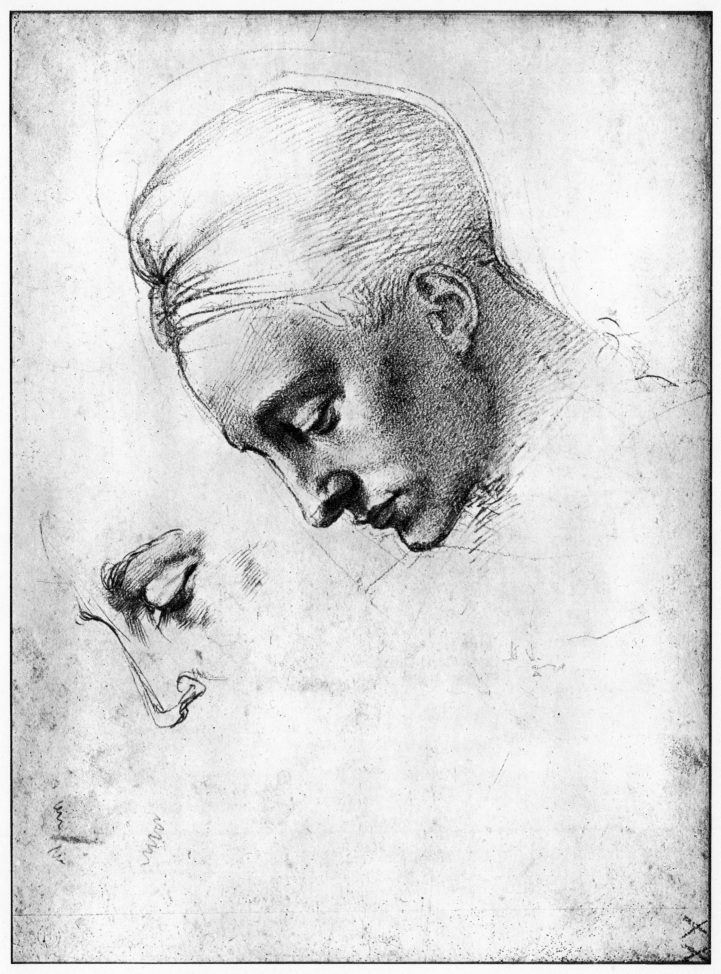

66. HEAD STUDY FOR THE 'LEDA' · 1530 · CASA BUONARROTI

67. SAMSON AND DELILAH · ABOUT 1530 · OXFORD

68. THREE LABOURS · OF HERCULES · ABOUT 1530 · WINDSOR

69. RUNNING SATYR · ABOUT 1530 · LOUVRE

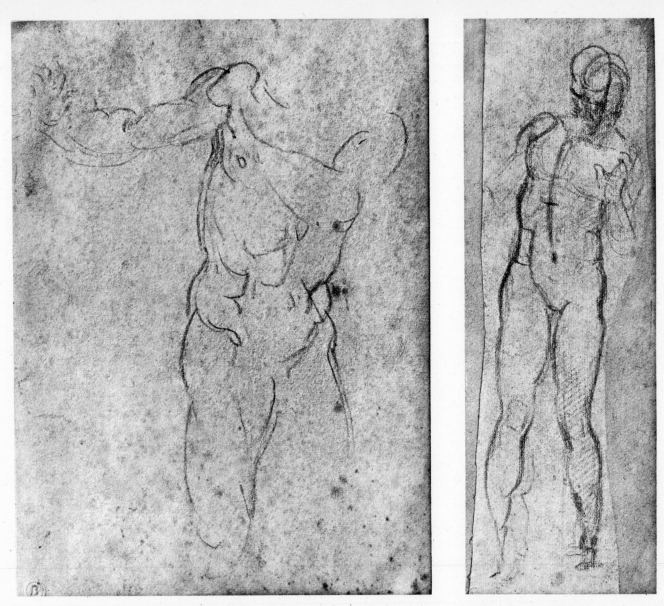

70-71. STUDIES FOR THE 'NOLI ME TANGERE' · 1531 · CASA BUONARROTI

72. STUDY FOR A FIGURE IN THE 'RESURRECTION OF CHRIST' · 1530-32 · CASA BUONARROTI

73. ARCHERS SHOOTING AT A HERM · 1530 · WINDSOR

74. TITYUS · 1532 · WINDSOR

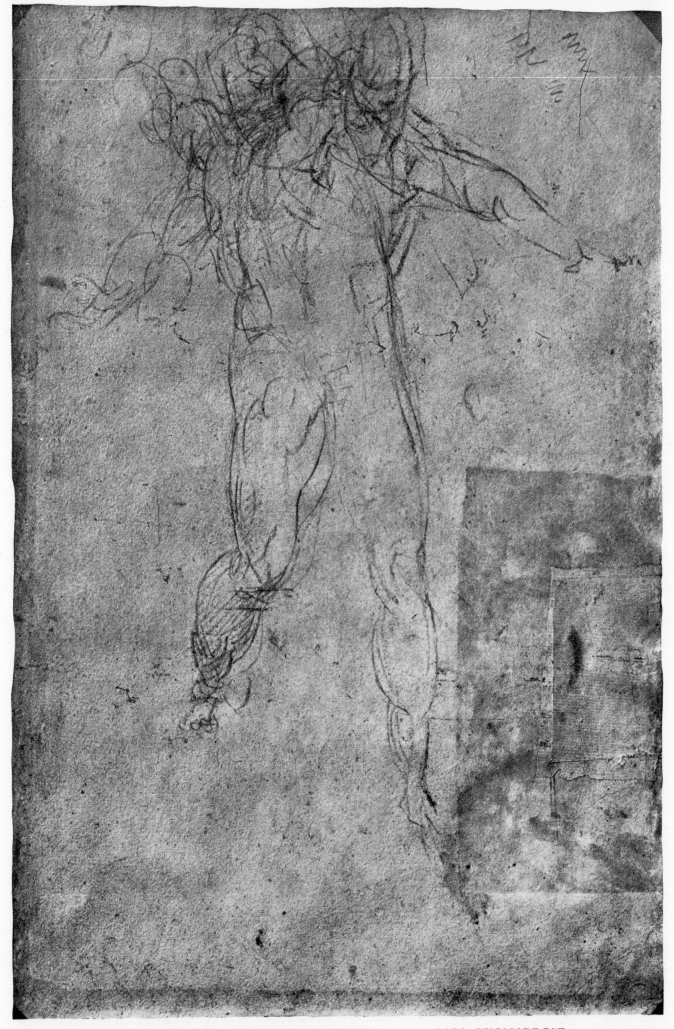

75. STUDY FOR THE 'RESURRECTION' · 1532 · CASA BUONARROTI

76. STUDY FOR THE 'RESURRECTION' · 1532 · CASA BUONARROTI

*77 · THE RESURRECTION · 1532 · LOUVRE

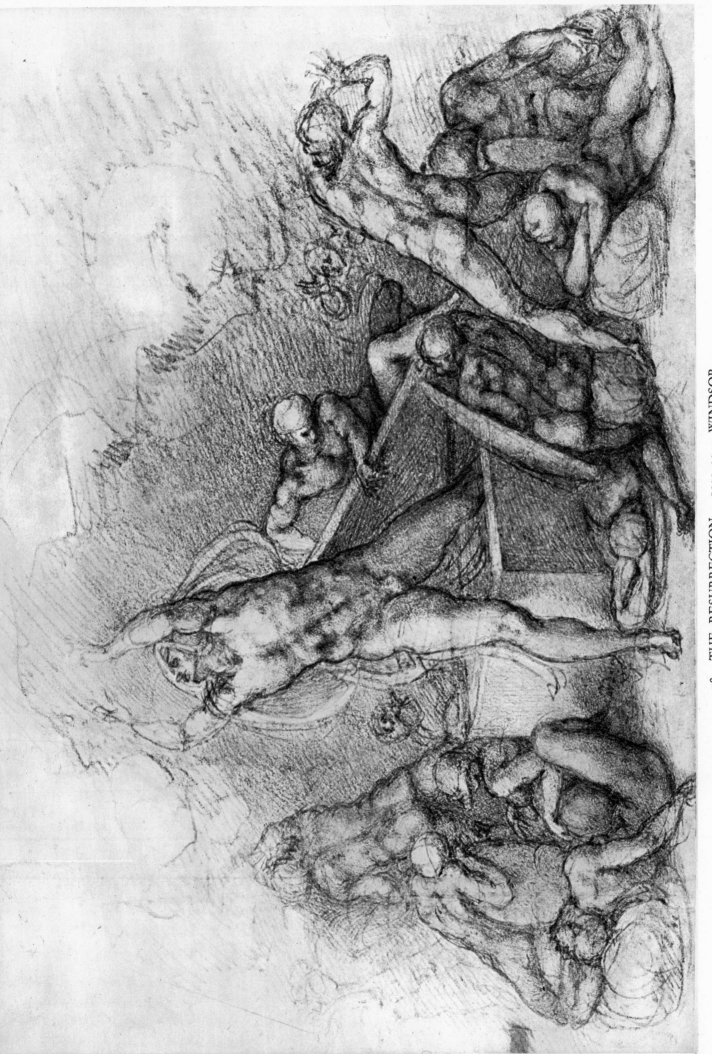

78.   THE RESURRECTION · 1532–33 · WINDSOR

92. BACCHANAL OF CHILDREN · ABOUT 1533 · WINDSOR

93. THE DREAM OF HUMAN LIFE · ABOUT 1533 · WEIMAR

94. THE FALL OF PHAËTHON · 1533 · BRITISH MUSEUM

95. THE FALL OF PHAËTHON · 1533 · VENICE

96. THE FALL OF PHAËTHON · 1533 · WINDSOR

97. ERIDANUS AND THE HELIADES · DETAIL OF No. 95

98. STUDY FOR THE 'LAST JUDGEMENT' · 1534 · BAYONNE

99. STUDY FOR THE 'LAST JUDGEMENT' · 1534 · BAYONNE

100. STUDY FOR THE 'LAST JUDGEMENT' · 1534 · CASA BUONARROTI

101. STUDY FOR THE 'LAST JUDGEMENT' · 1534 · BRITISH MUSEUM

118. CARTOON FOR A HOLY FAMILY · ABOUT 1542 · BRITISH MUSEUM

119. STUDIES FOR 'CHRIST TAKING LEAVE OF HIS MOTHER' · ABOUT 1542 · CAMBRIDGE

120. STUDY FOR A FIGURE UNDER THE
CROSS · ABOUT 1542 · LOUVRE

121. STUDY FOR A DRAPED FIGURE
ABOUT 1542 · OXFORD

122. THE VIRGIN OF THE ANNUNCIATION · ABOUT 1545 · BRITISH MUSEUM

*123. APOSTLE HOLDING A BOOK · ABOUT 1546–47 · HAARLEM

124. ANGEL, AND SKETCH FOR A PIETÀ · 1546–48 · BRITISH MUSEUM

125. CHRIST ON THE CROSS · ABOUT 1546-48 · OXFORD

126. ANNUNCIATION · ABOUT 1550 · BRITISH MUSEUM

127. ANNUNCIATION · AFTER 1556 · OXFORD

128. CHRIST ON THE CROSS · ABOUT 1556–58 · WINDSOR

129. CHRIST ON THE CROSS · ABOUT 1556-58 · BRITISH MUSEUM

*130. MOTHER AND CHILD · AFTER 1558 · BRITISH MUSEUM

APPENDIX

EXCURSUS I: TECHNICAL
EXCURSUS II: CRITICAL
TEXT ILLUSTRATIONS
PLATE NOS. 132–208

BIBLIOGRAPHY
INDEX OF COLLECTIONS

THE TECHNIQUE OF
MICHELANGELO'S DRAWINGS

THE FOLLOWING SHORT NOTES on drawing media would be superfluous were it not for the fact that the various catalogues of Michelangelo's drawings contain a number of misconceptions and errors revealing the existence of certain doubts concerning these matters.

All Michelangelo's drawings are on paper. One drawing in the Louvre, our No. 10, is described by Berenson (No. 1588) as being 'on parchment', but in reality this, too, is on ordinary cotton paper. The paper used by Michelangelo is white, sometimes with a light-grey and sometimes with a buff tint. Brownish paper he used only for cartoons (Nos. 117 and 118). Occasionally he also used a paper with a light green ground,[1] e.g. for No. 21.

As Michelangelo did not use silverpoint,[2] papers specially prepared for this technique do not come into question, or, to put it more accurately, if he did use a sheet of this kind, he made his drawing on the unprepared side (see, for example, No. 28—a head in black chalk, with silverpoint sketches by another hand on the back). The numerous drawings in silverpoint attributed to Michelangelo (e.g. Berenson, Figs. 617 and 686) are not, in my opinion, by him. In one or two other cases, in so far as the drawings in question are authentic, the description 'silverpoint' is erroneous (e.g. in the case of a drawing in the Albertina, Berenson No. 1606, our No. 83, which is not, as Thode and Berenson state, in silverpoint, but in black chalk[3]).

Michelangelo used the following drawing media: charcoal, lead-point, pen and ink, black limestone chalk, black artificial chalk and red chalk.

Only three of Michelangelo's works are in *charcoal*, these being our Nos. 42, 117 and 118.[4]

Lead-point (also called leaden stylus) is described by Cennini (Chapter 11) as follows: 'It is possible to draw with a lead-point on paper not prepared with bone-dust;[5] that is, with two parts of lead and one of tin, well beaten with a hammer.' Lead-point was used especially for preliminary drawings, for example, for the first stage of pen drawings. Lead-point lines can easily be erased with bread-crumbs. Preliminary drawing of this kind can be discerned in our Nos. 14 and 21. Pencil, i.e. graphite, was not used by Michelangelo or any other draughtsman of his time; where the term is used (e.g. Tolnay, Nos. 24, 25; Berenson, No. 1571, etc.) it is due to confusion with black chalk, or sometimes with lead-point.

Most of Michelangelo's *pen and ink drawings* are executed with a quill pen and gall ink. This ink was originally black or

dark brown, but has now invariably faded, in some of the drawings to an almost yellow tone (e.g. in No. 1). As a result of the development of rust owing to the iron content, the ink has often eaten its way through the paper when the lines are heavily drawn (e.g. in No. 44). This penetration of the paper by the ink is a proof that gall ink was used, and the term 'bistre' in reference to certain drawings (e.g. Tolnay, Nos. 96 and 106) is wrong. *Bistre ink* is made from chimney or lamp soot, has a warm brown colour and does not attack the paper. Only occasionally did Michelangelo use bistre (e.g. in No. 26).

Black and red chalks[6] were used by Michelangelo from the time of his sketches for the Sistine Chapel ceiling. Limestone chalk—matita nera, pietra nera or lapis—is a schist rich in carbon, which can be sawn up into sticks (of the same shape as modern pastel pencils). Cennini describes limestone chalk in his thirty-fourth chapter: 'I have found that a certain black stone which comes from Piedmont is good for drawing; it is soft and very black. As it is soft, it can be sharpened with a knife. You can draw with it as you please, the same as with charcoal.' Vasari, in his Life of Bandinelli, mentions black limestone chalk amongst the usual drawing materials of the period: 'He managed with dexterity the stylus and the pen and also the red and the black chalk (la matita rossa e nera); the last is a soft stone from the mountains of France, and when carefully pointed, enables the artist to execute drawings of great finesse.'

Artificial chalk—'crayon noir'—is made of lamp soot mixed with potter's earth and generally also with wax; it differs from limestone chalk in its greater softness and in the intensity of its black tone.[7]

Michelangelo used both kinds of black chalk, the artificial variety, however, only after 1530 (e.g. in Nos. 70, 74, 75, 76, 78, 79, 91, 93, 94, 95, 96, 105, 108, 109, 110, etc.). On many of these sheets (e.g. No. 79) the foundation draft of the drawing is in limestone chalk, while the strengthening of the outlines and shadows is done in artificial chalk. The same technique is used for the late 'Crucifixions' (e.g. No. 128).

Red chalk, i.e. haematite, was frequently used by Michelangelo from the time of his sketches for the Sistine Chapel ceiling. Red chalk can be used as a drawing medium in its natural form, but has two disadvantages, namely, that not a line can be erased and the drawing must be fixed, as otherwise the lines may easily become blurred. Light red chalk may be made darker by steeping it in a mixture of turpentine and olive oil.[8]

Michelangelo used both light and dark shades of red chalk, and also a terra-cotta shade, but not the brown variety, which was preferred by Rosso and other mannerists.

---

[1] Cennino Cennini, *The Book of Art*, translated from the Italian by Christiana J. Herringham, London, 1899, Chaps. 15 and 16; p. 14: 'Green tints are the most beautiful and most frequently used.'

[2] Cennini, Chaps. 7 and 8. Joseph Meder, *Die Handzeichnung, ihre Technik und Entwicklung*, 2nd edition, Vienna, 1923, p. 79 f. This book contains the most detailed discussion of all drawing media. To English readers I would recommend Charles de Tolnay, *History and Technique of Old Master Drawings*, New York, 1943.

[3] Prof. Dr. O. Benesch, Director of the Albertina in Vienna, was kind enough to check this for me.

[4] The authenticity of these three works is not generally acknowledged.

[5] Such a foundation is essential when drawing with silverpoint, as otherwise the silver would leave no mark on the paper.

[6] According to Vasari, Michelangelo used black chalk and charcoal, together with white lead for the heightening of the lights, in his Battle Cartoon. As the last remnant of the cartoon has been lost, it is impossible to say more about it.

[7] A recipe dating from the end of the eighteenth century recommends the use of one pound of colophony, one-quarter of an ounce of yellow wax, and one-quarter of an ounce of tallow, melted over a fire and mixed with soot; the resulting mass was then drawn off into reeds.

[8] It is unlikely that acids were used for making red chalk darker before the end of the eighteenth century.

A CRITICAL EXAMINATION OF
MICHELANGELO'S DRAWINGS

Jonson: So thou canst distinguish the false from the true?
Lister: I can, or I think I can, which is nearly the same thing.

GEORGE MOORE

THE question, how many genuine Michelangelo drawings there are, is one which can be answered either in an authoritative manner or else by reference to the bibliography of the subject. It seems to me that a reader who wishes to do more than merely enjoy the illustrations without questioning their authenticity, has a right to know how the author of this book arrived at his decisions, what he thinks of the opinions of other critics, and what doubts still linger in his mind. In other words, such a reader would like to know not only what are the opinions of myself and others, but also the whole process by which we arrived at them.

I think that in the Catalogue I have given a proper exposition of the pros and cons in the case of each drawing, so that, if the reader is not inclined to agree with me, he can easily extract his arguments from my references.

The drawings may be divided into two main groups— those having some connexion with works (either lost or extant) of Michelangelo, and those which are completely independent.

As regards the first group, we cannot assume *a priori* that such drawings were invariably preliminary studies; in a few cases it has been maintained—to my mind, wrongly—that Michelangelo made these sketches *after* the completion of the work. An example of this is said to be the 'Bruges Madonna' (Plate 20), which has been described as a 'memory sketch', while several drawings of figures in the Medici chapel are alleged to have been made *after* the respective models and not as a preparation for them (e.g. Plates 59 and 60).

As regards the remaining drawings in this group, in so far as their attribution to Michelangelo has been denied, the question remains whether they are copies after his frescoes, cartoons and sculptures, or copies of authentic drawings by his hand. To quote examples, if we wish to doubt the authenticity of Nos. 30 and 60, we cannot consider them to be copies of finished works, but must assume that they are copied from other drawings, since we have here to do with male models corresponding to female figures in the work as eventually executed. No. 102, on the other hand, and a number of similar drawings, can be explained as copies after frescoes. Although in my opinion No. 102 and other drawings of the kind are authentic, there exist nevertheless numerous drawings which are definitely copies of works executed by Michelangelo. Vasari gives us long lists of artists who copied the Battle Cartoon and made sketches in the Medici chapel;[1] we know that immediately after the completion of the 'Last Judgement', Venusti made sketches of parts of it, and of Battista Franco we are told that 'there did not ultimately remain a single design, or sketch, nay not even a copy executed by Michelangelo, that he did not make a copy from'.

Even on sheets containing authentic drawings by Michelangelo's hand, we frequently find copies and sketches by the hands of pupils, e.g. on Nos. 30, 34, 40 and 53 (*cf.* the Catalogue).

It is not always easy to decide, or at all events it is often questionable, whether certain sheets are originals or merely skilful copies. To this category belong Nos. 27, 62, 63, 70, 71, 76 and 112, all of which, in my opinion, are genuine. The presentation drawings were naturally favourite subjects for copyists, and although such copies are not difficult to detect, it has occurred that, during critical siftings of the drawings, several genuine works have been rejected. Nos. 49–51 have been deemed to be copies; likewise, quite wrongly, Nos. 73, 92, 93 and 113.

In the case of drawings connected with frescoes and sculptures, the dating is relatively certain, but even in such cases the certainty is often merely apparent. The most important point is whether the drawings have been correctly interpreted. No. 17, for example, was wrongly interpreted as 'Haman' (which would give a date about 1510); the group of three men in No. 20 was alleged to be connected with the Battle Cartoon (*i.e.* about 1504); No. 29 has been wrongly brought into relationship with the Doni Madonna (1504–06); hitherto no one has doubted that No. 33 was a 'study for the Sistine Chapel ceiling' (for which reason it has been wrongly dated 1508–10); No. 41 has been interpreted as a 'Head of Adam' (and therefore wrongly dated about 1508); Nos. 44–46 were supposed to be connected with the Battle Cartoon (*i.e.* about 1504); No. 56 was wrongly assumed to be a preliminary study for 'Haman' (about 1510); No. 66 to be a study for the Sistine Chapel ceiling (thus dating it twenty years too early); No. 70 to be a sketch for the 'Adam' in the 'Expulsion from Paradise' (likewise twenty years too early); No. 82 to be connected with the Medici Madonna (about eighteen years too early); No. 119 to contain studies for the 'Noli me tangere' (thus dating it wrongly 1531).

If we examine drawings such as Nos. 17, 29, 33, 41, 56, 66, 70 and 82 more closely, we see at once, without needing any further explanation, that Michelangelo remained faithful for long periods to old motives, so that studies for different works can be distinguished only by their style, not by their motives. This explains the false datings mentioned above.

Examples of the retention of motives are certain figures in the 'Last Judgement', which are developed out of the figures of Captives on the tomb of Julius, despite the interval of twenty-five years. It could also be shown that figures from the Battle Cartoon are found again, not only on the Sistine Chapel

---

[1] Among them Daniele da Volterra. Thode and other critics have attributed to him a partial copy of the Battle Cartoon (Plate 182). This attribution, which is justified, might serve as a starting-point for the assignation to the same artist, as copies after Michelangelo, of a number of doubtful drawings (e.g. Plate 183). (This, in fact, is one of the most difficult problems in the criticism of Michelangelo's drawings.) Daniele da Volterra made copies of other works by Michelangelo. In a letter to the master dated May 8, 1557, he confesses that he has been to the latter's house in the Via Mozza in Florence and there found just as much to copy as in Rome with all its antiquities (Frey, *Briefe*, No. 354).

ceiling, but also in the 'Last Judgement'. In the 'Conversion of St. Paul' (1546–50) we find figures related to those in Nos. 78 and 79 (about 1532).

Frequently Michelangelo deliberately developed out of one body motive a number of others. The outlines of Tityus (No. 74) are traced through on the back of the sheet (reproduced in *Italian Drawings at Windsor Castle*, p. 252), thus forming a first sketch for the Risen Christ. This figure, very similar in its movement to the Haman on the Sistine Chapel ceiling, then underwent further development (Nos. 76–81) and was eventually transformed into the Christ of the 'Last Judgement' (Nos. 99, 100). This Christ, very similar to the Zeus of the Phaëthon (Nos. 94, 95), then underwent a final metamorphosis into the Christ of the 'Cleansing of the Temple' (Nos. 105, 108–110). To cite another example, the lower part of the body of the man in the 'Bacchanal of Children' (No. 92) is copied from a figure in the 'Resurrection' (Nos. 77, 78), while the upper part of the body is found again in the Colonna Pietà (Plate 138).[2]

That Michelangelo himself often varied his motives, must have made the work of forgers much easier (Thode, II, p. 18; Tolnay, I, p. 255). Malvasia mentions that copies in black and red chalk after the 'Last Judgement' were shown to Denys Calvart (1540–1619), in Cardinal Alessandro d'Este's collection of drawings, as originals, which, however, as he explained to the Cardinal, he had made himself, 'altering the figures at certain points'.[3] Another forger, as we learn from a letter written by Roselli to Michelangelo in 1525, was Giuliano Leni, while many of Battista Franco's copies after Michelangelo seem to have been made with the intention of passing them off as genuine (Robinson, *The Drawings by Michelangelo . . . in Oxford*, p. 322). One of the dealers who (about 1580) engaged in the sale of forged Michelangelo drawings was a certain Pomponio. He used a method which he may even have learned from Michelangelo himself;[4] he made the paper thinner at certain points and then exposed the drawing to the effects of smoke. Forgeries of another kind are reproduced by Berenson (*Drawings of Florentine Painters*, 1938, Figs. 601, 789, 792, 833).

It is understandable that in such circumstances an exaggerated cautiousness was displayed towards unusual Michelangelo drawings and that some critics should have rejected genuine works as forgeries. For instance, the studies for the 'Adam' and the 'Haman' in the British Museum and the 'Labours of Hercules' at Windsor Castle have been held to be forgeries. Certain other drawings, too, if their authenticity is not to be admitted, must be considered as forgeries, since their technique excludes the possibility that they can be copies—e.g. Nos. 54–56, 62, and 102, which, however, in my opinion are all genuine.

A number of drawings are accredited by inscriptions in Michelangelo's handwriting, some of these being drawings connected with sculptures and frescoes and others independent of such works. It is, of course, just as easy to copy or forge

handwriting as it is drawings,[5] but connoisseurs display less mistrust towards handwriting.

Only rarely do these inscriptions refer to the drawings themselves, e.g. No. 9, which bears the inscription 'David with the Sling', etc.; No. 35, on which two lines of handwriting stress the fact that this is a drawing by Michelangelo's own hand; No. 53, on which the master advises his pupil Mini to copy the sketches of the Madonna; No. 57, on which are certain instructions to the stonemason; No. 94, on which he asks Cavalieri about further work on the composition. On the front or back of other drawings[6] are verses and notes of all kinds (Nos. 6, 7, 17, 19, 22, 23, 24, 34, 37, 44, 45, 53, 83, 127).

Other drawings exist on which only part of the handwriting is Michelangelo's, the remainder being in another hand (e.g. Nos. 21 and 31, on which only one line was written by Michelangelo). An interesting example of this is Plate 134, containing writing by both Michelangelo and his pupil Mini, the sketch on the sheet being also by Mini. Plate 134 shows that the presence of Michelangelo's handwriting on a sheet is not a definite proof that the drawing is authentic.

On the other hand, taking as starting-points dated specimens or such as can easily be dated, Michelangelo's handwriting provides a good means of dating drawings, since it underwent clearly distinguishable changes during the various stages of his career.[7]

During Michelangelo's lifetime many of his drawings were given wider circulation in the form of engravings, and among these are those important engravings reproducing drawings which have been lost (Plates 136, 138, 139 and 142). It need hardly be said that a drawing is not necessarily genuine merely because it agrees with some such engraving, and that quality is the only criterion for deciding whether we have before us an original or a copy (see Nos. 93 and 113 in the Catalogue).

A composition which until recently was known only through old engravings (and a few very free copies in oil painting), and of which the original drawing is said to have now come to light, is *The Holy Family*, called *Il Silenzio*, now in the possession of the Duke of Portland (Plate 141).[8] This drawing passed through a number of celebrated collections, and its origin can be traced

---

[2] This reminds us of Thomas Mann's remark about Goethe: 'Even the world of so mighty a mind, wide though it may be, is but a closed, a limited world, an entity, in which motives repeat themselves and the same images recur again at long intervals.'

[3] The presence of *pentimenti*, too, which is generally held to be a definite proof of authenticity, sometimes requires investigation; it is obvious that a clever forger (or copyist) would not fail to make use of this convenient method of giving an impression of genuineness.

[4] See Introduction, p. 10.

[5] A delightful example of this, which has escaped the notice of art historians, probably because the source is amusing, is related by Casanova in his memoirs. At Aix-en-Provence in 1768 he met Cagliostro, who showed him various copies he had made, among them one of a Rembrandt drawing, 'if anything, more beautiful than the original'. Eventually Casanova gave Cagliostro a letter of recommendation to a banker in Avignon. This letter was returned to Casanova the same evening, and in response to a direct inquiry he identified it as the original, whereas, as Cagliostro afterwards told him, it was only a copy, in other words, a forgery. 'Your talent is marvellous,' said Casanova to Cagliostro; 'it is far more difficult to imitate handwriting than it is to imitate a drawing. With that gift you will go far.'

[6] When the inscription is not visible in the reproductions in the present volume, this means that it is on the back of the sheet—see the text to each number in the Catalogue.

[7] These changes can be followed if we examine the inscribed sheets listed above. Three specimens of his signature are also reproduced in the present volume—on Plate 9 (1502), Plate 133 (1524) and on p. 20 (after 1558). To the specimens of handwriting reproduced on the plates or in the Catalogue must be added Plate 132 (*ca.* 1510) and Plate 135 (1552). The relationship between the character of the handwriting at various periods and the ductus of the line, especially in pen-drawings, is a matter the explanation of which would require a special volume to itself. Nevertheless, with the help of the scanty material here presented and his own perception, the reader should be able to work out the elementary principles of this comparative method.

[8] Holbein Exhibition (No. 276), Royal Academy, London, December, 1950–March, 1951.

back to the Casa Buonarroti. Nevertheless, there remains the question, susceptible only of a subjective answer, whether this drawing comes up to the high standard which it ought to have if it is to be accepted as an original.

Another very tricky question, just as difficult as that of the 'quality', is the relationship between antique sculptures and motives in Michelangelo's drawings. Many attempts to establish these relationships have been made by scholars.[9] One of the most important discoveries of this kind we owe to Wilde, namely, that an antique relief belonging to Lorenzo Ghiberti's descendants, the so-called 'Bed of Polycletus', was frequently used as a model by Michelangelo and his school. In this volume I have included the first good reproductions of the Mattei relief and of Tribolo's mosaic, and also a few other examples (Plates 143–146). Another antique sculpture, the 'Dying Niobid', also enjoyed a great reputation during the sixteenth century.[10] The best reproduction, dating from the time when the sculpture was still in the Casa Maffei, is to be found in two details of a drawing by Perino del Vaga (Plates 162, 163).[11] The motive of this Niobid was copied exactly by Michelangelo (Plate 164), though reversed as if seen in a mirror.[12]

Another, hitherto unnoticed case of the use of an antique work exists with the figure of the falling Phaëthon (see illustrations below).

In many other cases the meticulously elaborated relation-

ships between Michelangelo drawings and antique models are not very convincing.[13]

Another problem of which at least the outlines should be investigated, is that of the influence exercised by contemporary artists and immediate predecessors on Michelangelo, and also the question whether these influences can be traced back to the imitation of antique works of art. The fact that Michelangelo copied works of Giotto, Masaccio, Schongauer and Giovanni Pisano is generally known. The influence of Donatello, Jacopo della Quercia, and perhaps even of Rogier van der Weyden and Dürer, may also be admitted, although this hardly helps us to explain anything in Michelangelo's art. More important is the elucidation of Michelangelo's relationship to Raphael and Leonardo in certain specific instances.

One case which, it seems to me, would repay investigation concerns the presentation drawing for Perini, the 'Damned Soul' (No. 49). It has been repeatedly asserted that the inspiration for this came from a screaming head in Leonardo's Battle Cartoon. But this head of Leonardo's can be traced back to Verrocchio, and is found again in the form of a shouting soldier in the Resurrection relief from the Villa Careggi,[14] and also as a Medusa on a terra-cotta bust of Giuliano de' Medici (Plate 166).[15] It appears once again as a Medusa in a drawing by Raphael (Plate 167). The first link in this chain was undoubtedly an antique Medusa mask which was presumably in the collection of antiques at the Casino Mediceo, but it remains uncertain whether Michelangelo drew the inspiration for his drawing (Plate 168) directly from this antique Medusa, or whether it came to him indirectly through Leonardo and Verrocchio, or through Raphael.

A second instance likewise leads us to the domain of Raphael. No. 58 is held to be an independent sketch for one of the river gods in the Medici chapel. If, however, we compare this sketch (Plate 152) with the nymph in the Raphael engraving (Plate 149) of the 'Judgement of Paris'—the characteristic common to both is the way in which one leg is tucked in and drawn up—we begin to doubt the independence of Michelangelo's sketch and to ask ourselves whether the inspiration came from Raphael or whether both artists used an antique sculpture as model. The latter supposition is strengthened if we examine the river god in the Raphael engraving (Plate 149), the movement of which corresponds with the Venus in Michelangelo's composition of 1532 (Plate 150, and the sketch reproduced on p. 178).[16] In this case a drawing made from the

---

[9] See, among others, items 43 and 46 in the Bibliography.

[10] Until 1540 the statue was in the Casa Maffei in Rome, and after that in the Palazzo Bevilacqua in Verona. A drawing made after the statue is to be found in the 'Wolfegger Skizzenbuch' (Fol. 33 v., attributed to Amico Aspertini; Fürstlich Waldburgsche Bibliothek); another, smaller reproduction is in Marten van Heemskerck's sketchbook (Fol. 3 v., about 1535; Berlin, Print Room); a third, by Figino, is at Windsor Castle (Cat. No. 326–23 r.). The sculpture itself is now in the Glyptothek at Munich (Plate 164). There is another version in the Uffizi.

[11] Formerly in the collection of Richard Cosway, now in that of Pietro del Giudice, London. Most of the other sketches on this sheet reproduce sculptures belonging to Cardinal Andrea della Valle (1463–1534).

[12] In addition to antique Niobid figures, Michelangelo also used mediæval representations of St. Sebastian and of the Flagellation as models for his Captives. Fettered figures such as Michelangelo planned for the tomb of Julius are also found among Leonardo's sketches for the Trivulzio equestrian statue (1511). See also illustrations on p. 179.

(a)   (b)

(a) Detail from an antique marble group, called 'Hector and Troilus', formerly in the Farnese Collection, Rome (now Naples, Museo Nazionale, No. 150). From an engraving in F. Perrier's 'Segmenta nobilium signorum et statuarum', Rome, 1638.
(b) 'Phaëthon', detail from Michelangelo's drawing, Plate 94.

[13] E. Petersen, in Zeitschrift für bildende Kunst, 1898, p. 294 f., relates an Etruscan fresco in Corneto, representing a 'Hades head', to a drawing attributed to Michelangelo in the Archivio Buonarroti (Cod. XIII, fol. 40 B; Frey, Dichtungen, p. 384 f.). H. Bulle, F. Weege and many other scholars agree with him on this point. The Etruscan head, however, is wearing a cap of dog- or wolf-skin, whereas the head in the drawing is covered by a boar's head. This fact alone brings the drawing into closer relationship with the standard-bearers on the Column of Trajan than with the Etruscan 'Hades'. The crux of the matter is, however, that this drawing is not by Michelangelo at all, but by Montelupo, as can be seen if we compare it with Plate 194, in which a similar animal's head, executed in exactly the same technique, can be seen above the mask. There are scores of other postulated relationships between Michelangelo and antique art that would not bear a close examination.

[14] Florence, Museo Nazionale; about 1465–70. Some critics think that the young Leonardo had a share in this work.

[15] National Gallery, Washington, Mellon Collection, No. A–16.

[16] Even if we assume that Michelangelo's Venus is merely a variant of one of his own river-god sketches, this does not alter the chronology. Raphael made use of the motive about 1512, Michelangelo about 1530, ten years after Raphael's death.

Sketch for 'Venus and Cupid', pen and ink drawing, 1531–32.
British Museum (BB. 1504).

antique model has been preserved—the drawing of a Hercules torso in the Ambrosiana, generally attributed to Sebastiano del Piombo.[17]

The Hercules in Raphael's Farnesina frescoes likewise corresponds partially[18] with Michelangelo's sketch for the river god (Plates 151, 152).

I believe that in all the above-mentioned cases antique sculptures were the models; but I am convinced that Michelangelo learned the use of them from Raphael.[19]

Michelangelo's Christ in Santa Maria sopra Minerva (Plates 36 and 155) likewise seems to owe something to Raphael. The characteristic feature of the movement (namely, the arm thrown diagonally across the breast and the head turned towards the other side) was borrowed by Raphael himself from Leonardo (Plates 153 and 154).

Michelangelo's relationship to Leonardo is far more transparent than his relationship to Raphael. It is generally agreed that the drawing of St. Anne with the Virgin and Child (No. 8) is a copy after Leonardo.[20] Conversely, on two occasions Leonardo copied Michelangelo (Plates 160, 161), namely, the marble David (1504) and the Moses (1515).[21] In copying the David, he prepared the way for its transformation into a Neptune by adding sea-horses. Leonardo's drawing of 'Neptune in his Sea-chariot' (Plate 156) is only slightly later than his copy of Michelangelo's David.

With this drawing of Neptune, however, the problem begins to grow complicated. Firstly, the movement motive of Leonardo's Neptune is found again in the Zeus of Michelangelo's Phaëthon (Plate 95) and in his 'Risen Christ' (Plate 159). The borrowing here strikes the eye, but at the same time

it is questionable. And that constitutes the second part of the problem.

From an old report we learn that a similar Neptune composition by Michelangelo in red chalk also existed.[22] An inscription on this drawing stated that it first belonged to Giovanni Paolo Lomazzo and later (1578) to Giovanni Ambrogio Figino. This drawing, however, cannot be identified with the Leonardo drawing at Windsor Castle (Plate 156), since the latter is not in red, but in black chalk, and does not contain the above-mentioned inscription. On the other hand, we have proof that Figino really owned this red-chalk drawing by Michelangelo, for he repeatedly copied it (e.g. in Plate 157).[23] The Neptune in Figino's copy is akin to several other figures of Michelangelo's, to the Christ in the 'Last Judgement' and the Christ in the 'Expulsion from the Temple'. As, however, Michelangelo's Neptune drawing has disappeared and the date of its creation is unknown, the only facts we can establish are that Leonardo, on the basis of Michelangelo's David, designed a Neptune (Plate 160); that Michelangelo himself, at the same time or later, designed a 'Neptune driving his Sea-horses', and that Leonardo did likewise (Plates 156, 157). At all events the relationship between Leonardo and Michelangelo must here have been very close, for the starting-point—a very curious one for a Neptune composition—was Michelangelo's statue of David.[24]

We must now consider as briefly as possible the relationship between Michelangelo and his pupils and imitators, that is to say, those drawings which have wrongly been eliminated from Michelangelo's œuvre and assigned to pupils, or conversely.

His relationship to Bacchiacca is discussed in the Catalogue under No. 65, that to Mini under Nos. 53 and 67 (see also Plates 134 and 207). Most important of all is Michelangelo's relationship to Sebastiano del Piombo and Daniele da Volterra, since this affects a whole series of very beautiful drawings by Michelangelo which have been wrongly ascribed to these two pupils. It is a sad blow to the credit of the 'contractionists' that some of these drawings (e.g. Nos. 89 and 114) are alternately attributed to Sebastiano and to Daniele, which appears incomprehensible and inexcusable when we compare the absolutely certain drawings of Sebastiano and Daniele with one another, and note that they have no relationship whatsoever.[25] If the critics who are so anxious to deprive Michelangelo of beautiful drawings like the 'Deposition' in Haarlem and the

---

[17] Pallucchini, *Sebastian Viniziano*, Plate 90 B; O. Fischel, in *Old Master Drawings*, 1939–40, 'A new approach to Sebastiano del Piombo', Fig. 17–18.

[18] Namely, in the position of the legs. For the upper part of the body Raphael used the Belvedere torso, just as Michelangelo did—about seven years later—for the 'Giorno' in the Medici chapel.

[19] In the use of the antique relief known as the 'Bed of Polycletus', on the other hand, the priority is Michelangelo's. Raphael used a figure from this relief—but not the same one as Michelangelo—for his Farnesina frescoes (Fischel, *Raphael*, I, London, 1948, p. 12).

[20] As regards the studies of putti, see the Catalogue text to No. 19; for the sketch of the Battle of Horsemen, the text to No. 22; and for the 'Captives', the text to No. 32.

[21] A. Venturi, *Studi dal Vero*, 1927, p. 59 ('il tipo di Mosè vendicatore'); W. R. Valentiner in *Burlington Magazine*, Vol. XCI, 1949, p. 343.

[22] See Thode, V, p. 375. Giovanni Gaetano Bottari, *Raccolta di Lettere sulla Pittura*, VI, 247 (1768).

[23] Just as Leonardo's Neptune was used as model for bronzes (Vienna, Museum, and London, Beit Collection), so Michelangelo's Neptune would seem to have been given plastic form, for in his drawings Figino shows Neptune and his horses seen from various angles. It is assumed that the motive of all the Renaissance Neptune bronzes derives 'from the antique', but the prototype has not yet been traced.

[24] Giovanni Carrara, who in 1768 was the owner of the Neptune drawing attributed to Michelangelo, thought that it was a design for a fountain. E. Moeller (1926) declared that Leonardo's copy of the 'David' was likewise a design for a fountain.

[25] For Sebastiano del Piombo, see the Catalogue text to Nos. 40, 86–89, and Plates 39–41, 43, 80, 86–90, 114, 122. See also Berenson, *Drawings of the Florentine Painters*, 1938, I, pp. 239–250.
For Daniele da Volterra, see Bibliography, item 63, and Plates 85, 114, 123, 126.
The following drawings have been attributed to Daniele da Volterra—By Panofsky: BB.1471, 2480, 2486. By Baumgart: BB.1402, 1403, 1409, 1417, 1514, 1534, 1577, 1600, 1702. By Wilde: BB.1470 and 2480 *verso*. By Berenson: BB.1653. Of these, BB.1417, 1470, 1534, 2480 *recto* and 2486 are, to my mind, by Michelangelo. Of the others, only very few are by Daniele da Volterra—but it is my task here to define Michelangelo's work as a draughtsman, and not that of Daniele da Volterra.

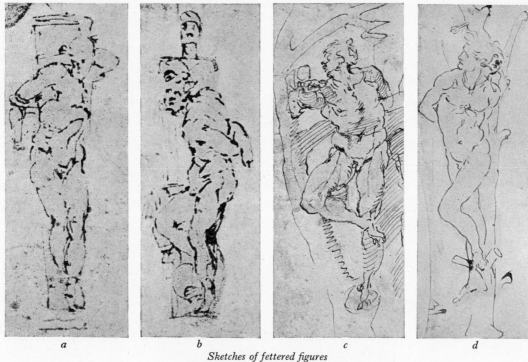

a   *b*   *c*   *d*

Sketches of fettered figures
(*a* and *b*) by Michelangelo: Details of Plate 32.
(*c*) by Michelangelo: Detail of Plate 56.
(*d*) by Leonardo da Vinci: St. Sebastian. (Hamburg, Kunsthalle)
See footnote 24 on p. 32

Warwick Pietà in the British Museum, cannot agree as to whether they are by Sebastiano or by Daniele, that does not by any means prove that they are not by Michelangelo, but rather that the critics have an undefined idea of the draughtsmanship of both Sebastiano and Daniele.

If we take the well-authenticated drawings of Daniele as a starting-point (Plates 184, 186), we find that a sketch in Oxford, Plate 187, corresponds pretty well with Plate 184, as do also some obscure little studies (e.g. Plates 188–190). The drawing on Plate 185, which is very close to that on Plate 184, reveals, on further examination, differences not only in the quality, but also in the ductus of the chalk-strokes. In the case of Plate 185, the figures adhere to one another, the legs are drawn badly, with staccato lines, whereas on Plate 184 everything is effortless, drawn with a feeling for plasticity and depth, like a drawing after a relief.

Baumgart made the drawing on Plate 191 the starting-point of his attributions, but in my opinion it is not by Daniele, but by an anonymous Mannerist, to whom I also attribute the drawing on Plate 192.

We have already seen above (p. 175 and Note 1) that both Daniele da Volterra and Battista Franco made numerous copies of Michelangelo's drawings. It may therefore be assumed that in a number of drawings both Franco and Daniele came so close to Michelangelo's style that their works may easily be confused with his.

The question, which of Franco's drawings have been wrongly attributed to Michelangelo, can be easily answered if we accept the opinion of H. Voss (*Malerei der Spätrenaissance in Rom und Florenz*, p. 118), namely, that the figure study in Oxford, Plate 203, is an independent preliminary sketch by Franco for one of his paintings. If we do not accept this, the problem becomes complicated. Characteristic of the Oxford drawing are the regular, thin, parallel hatching lines, the softness and bone-

lessness of the figures and their unsteady pose. Taking this drawing as our starting-point, we may attribute to Franco other drawings in the same style (e.g. Plate 202). Very similar in technique is also the head with the Phrygian cap in Oxford (Plate 200), and closely related to the latter head is the much-discussed head of a Faun in the Louvre (Plate 199). The attribution of a study of a head in red chalk (Plate 201) is likely to be less disputed, but this drawing—apart from the different material used—does not differ so very much from the two heads mentioned above, and even resembles them in certain Morellian details such as the shape of the ear. In pen drawings more pronouncedly Venetian in style, Franco produces a completely different effect, and this is particularly true when he indulges in flourishes, such drawings being reminiscent of Cambiaso (Plate 204).[26] In order to give a further characterization of Franco's linear technique, I have also reproduced a large detail from the 'Prudence' (Plate 196), as a contrast to a mask of Montelupo's (Plate 197)[27], and another mask-like head (Plate 198) which I think may be attributed to Cosini, that assistant of Michelangelo who executed the frieze of masks in the Medici chapel.

Michelangelo's 'Ricordi' contain a vast number of names of the master's assistants and pupils, and one may assume that they all, at one time or another, came so close to Michelangelo's style that their works were mistaken, or are still mistaken, for his. In addition to this, we have the 'Michelangelo school', that is to say, his imitators. The names of these pupils, assistants

[26] The drawing we discussed first, that on Plate 203, was indeed attributed by Morelli to Cambiaso.

[27] Montelupo's pen drawings are easily recognizable, as he was left-handed. Bandinelli's drawings, often very similar, are no longer confused with Michelangelo's. Likewise there is no difficulty in recognizing the coarse technique of Mini and Passerotti (Plates 207, 208).

and imitators are known, but ideas as to their style of drawing are either non-existent or very vague. Some of them have already been mentioned, and below we give a further excerpt from the list: Piero di Giannotto (about 1500); Lapo (after 1506); the sculptor Pietro Urbano (about 1508–21); Michi, Giovanni, Bernardino di Pier Basso (about 1510); Silvio Falcone, Rinieri, Cecho (after 1513); and during the later period Montorsoli, Calcagni, Venusti and Ammanati.

No drawing has yet been found by Francesco Urbino (who began in 1542 as Michelangelo's colour-grinder, was for thirteen years his servant and his assistant in his house, and is known to have executed paintings). The same may be said of Condivi, and also of Frizzi (who collaborated in the finishing of the Christ in Santa Maria sopra Minerva). Nor have we any drawings by the other assistants mentioned above.[28]

We possess at least one drawing (Plate 147) which is certainly by Tribolo, and taking this as a basis we can attribute other drawings to this artist (e.g. Plate 148). One interesting design for a fountain (Plate 195; in the Louvre, amongst Michelangelo's drawings), is, I am convinced, by Ammanati. An arm study inscribed 'dos reales' (Plate 194), is probably by Alonso Berruguete, that 'young Spaniard', whom Michelangelo in 1508 recommended to his brother Buonarroto in a letter, and who also copied the master's Battle Cartoon. A drawing in the British Museum (Plate 193), until recently held to be by Michelangelo himself, is now rightly attributed to Pierino da Vinci. As regards Rosso Fiorentino's drawings, too, critics are, on the whole, agreed (e.g. Plate 174, which Thode believed to be an authentic drawing of Michelangelo's).

If it is a question of identifying any one pupil or imitator of Michelangelo and gradually attributing to him a small œuvre, then all the above-mentioned names are available and many others as well! The National Gallery in London possesses two Michelangelesque paintings—a Madonna and Child with St. John and Angels (called 'The Manchester Madonna') and an Entombment. As long ago as 1891 Wölfflin recognized both these works as imitations in the style of Michelangelo. Naturally attempts were made to identify the imitator—as Mini (A. E. Popp), as Bugiardini (Berenson), as Jacopino del Conte (A. Venturi) and as Battista Franco (F. Antal). Some of the critics attributed both the paintings to the same imitator, others to two different artists, while some even added other paintings, not all of them obviously by the same hand, to the œuvre. Such attempts at identification merely demonstrate the presence of heterogeneous elements in the work of the 'Master of the Manchester Madonna'.[29] On the other hand, it has been possible rightly to attribute to him two drawings previously held to be by Michelangelo—those on Plate 179 (Popp) and Plate 176 (Baumgart). Taking his chief work, the 'Manchester Madonna' (Plate 177), as a starting-point, I also attribute to this anonymous master the celebrated coloured drawing of the Madonna in Florence (Plate 178), which in the opinion of Thode and Brinckmann is by Michelangelo himself, whereas Berenson attributes it to Bugiardini. If, alternatively, we take as our basis the pen drawing in the Louvre (Plate 179), then a whole series of other drawings (curiously enough, almost all of them in the Louvre) can be attributed to him (e.g. Plates 180 and 181).

In his efforts to reconstruct the œuvre of another anonymous imitator, Baumgart (*Die Jugendzeichnungen Michelangelos*, p. 37) took as one of his bases a poor study in the Louvre (Plate 205), and deprived Michelangelo of two vaguely similar, but autograph, drawings (Plates 54 and 55) in order to assign them to this artist. I do not wish to disparage the acuteness of Baumgart's perception, nevertheless I cannot accept his starting-point. In addition to chalk sketches, the Louvre sheet also contains a pen drawing (reproduced by itself as Plate 205), and if we compare this detail with the above-mentioned two Madonna studies (Plates 54, 55, and perhaps Plate 56 as well), we see that the outlines on Plate 205 look as if they were made of wire, and we can also detect notable weaknesses in the details, e.g. in the formation of the right foot. It is precisely in these details that Plate 55 is outstandingly good and differs in no wise from the drawing on Plate 53, which nobody has thought of doubting. The outlines, too, on Plates 54, 55 and 56, are drawn with undulating strokes of the pen, with a feeling for plastic values and the effect of depth; whereas the sketch on Plate 205 is closely related to a drawing in the Albertina, which A. E. Popham (*Burlington Magazine*, LXXXVI, 1945, p. 89 f.) attributes, with adequate reasons, to Perino del Vaga.

To investigate the work of the more distant imitators of Michelangelo would require a separate volume of considerable dimensions. Here I will only mention a cartoon by Taddeo Zuccaro (Plates 169 and 170), formerly held to be a work of Michelangelo's.[30] A study of draperies in the British Museum (Plate 172), where it is to be found among the genuine drawings by Michelangelo, seems to me to be also by Taddeo Zuccaro (*cf.* Plate 171), freely copied from the figure of a Sibyl on the Sistine ceiling.

---

[28] Berenson attributes the reverse of No. 2480 (our No. 89) to Pietro Urbano; Panofsky and Wilde, however, give it to Daniele da Volterra.

[29] Unfortunately, the case is more complicated than it would appear from my simple notes. There is actually no generally accepted basis for a discussion of the 'Master of the Manchester Madonna' because

Toesca (1934), Sir Kenneth Clark (1938) and Bertini (1945) ascribe the 'Entombment' and the 'Madonna' at the National Gallery to Michelangelo himself. They date the paintings very early, between 1502 and 1506, but they have offered no explanation of how it comes about that a Michelangelo drawing of a later date (BB.2503, of about 1533) was used in the 'Entombment'. (Cf. Tolnay, 17, pp. 236 and 265; Bertini, 15, pp. 47–49 and 57–58; Carl Justi, *Michelangelo, Neue Beiträge* Berlin, 1909.)

[30] This has been pointed out by Dr. Victor Bloch, Oxford.

132–135. *Michelangelo's Handwriting.*—132. Sonnet, describing Michelangelo's physical difficulties in painting the first section of the Sistine Ceiling frescoes (Frey IX). About 1510. Archivio Buonarroti.—133. Ricordo, dated 6 January 1523 (old style, i.e. 1524). Casa Buonarroti.—

134. Verso of a drawing with lines by Michelangelo and writing of Antonio Mini and his sketch of a baby (Frey 35A; BB. 1593 verso). About 1527. Louvre.—135. Michelangelo's most famous sonnet (Frey CXLVII). 1552. Codex Vaticanus.

BIBLIOGRAPHY OF
MICHELANGELO DRAWINGS

The following list of books and articles is intentionally kept concise, in order to help the student to find the most important titles first. Some further articles are quoted in the Catalogue of the present volume. There is a complete Michelangelo Bibliography in Vols. I and VIII of the *Römische Forschungen* of the Biblioteca Hertziana in Rome—*Michelangelo-Bibliographie* by E. Steinmann and R. Wittkower (1927), and a continuation by H. W. Schmidt in *Michelangelo im Spiegel seiner Zeit* (1930). For publications after 1930, see *Art Index*, New York, 1929 f.; and Cherubelli, *Supplemento alla bibliografia michelangiolesca*, 1931–1942. Florence, 1942.

I. COMPLETE CATALOGUES · REPRODUCTIONS SELECTIONS

1. Karl Frey, *Die Handzeichnungen Michelagniolos Buonarroti*, 3 vols. Berlin, 1909–11. (Publication of 300 drawings in two volumes with one volume of critical text).

2. Fritz Knapp, *Erster Nachtragsband* (zu Frey's Corpus). Berlin, 1925. (First supplement, containing the Haarlem drawings.)

2A. *Zweiter Nachtragsband*. Berlin, n.d. (This second supplementary volume contains 45 plates without text.)

3. Henry Thode, *Michelangelo und das Ende der Renaissance*, 3 vols. (Vol. I, 1902; II, 1903; III, 1912). *Michelangelo, Kritische Untersuchungen*, 3 vols. (Vol. I, 1908; II, 1908; III, 1913). The last three are referred to as Thode IV–VI. Volume VI, the most important one for our purposes, is listed separately as the following item.

3A. Henry Thode, *Michelangelo, Kritische Untersuchungen über seine Werke*, Vol. III: *Verzeichnis der Zeichnungen, Kartons und Modelle*. Berlin, 1913. (A very full list with short notes, often contradicting Frey. This volume is identical with Vol. VI of the complete work—see No. 3.)

4. Bernhard Berenson, *The Drawings of the Florentine Painters*, Amplified Edition, 3 vols. Chicago, 1938. (Contains an indispensable catalogue of the Michelangelo drawings. Several copies and imitations are listed under the name of the master, while a number of genuine drawings can be found under the names of Mini, 'Andrea di Michelangelo', and Sebastiano del Piombo.)

5. Michelangelo, *Disegni*. Istituto di edizioni artistiche, Fratelli Alinari. Florence, n.d. (1920 f.).

6. Erwin Panofsky, *Handzeichnungen Michelangelos*. Leipzig, 1922. (Twenty drawings with an excellent introduction.)

7. A. E. Brinckmann, *Michelangelo-Zeichnungen*. Munich, 1925. (Reproduces and discusses 83 drawings of which 20 are not by Michelangelo. The appendix contains 14 drawings which the author calls copies and imitations; but J. Wilde claims six of them for Michelangelo.)

7A. Anny E. Popp, *Review of Brinckmann's book*, in *Belvedere* (Forum), VIII, p. 72 f. Vienna, 1925.

8. Maurice Delacre, *Le Dessin de Michel-Ange*. Brussels, 1938.

9. Charles Rogers, *A Collection of Prints in Imitation of Drawings*. London, 1778.

10. William Young Ottley, *The Italian School of Design*. London, 1823.

There are quite a number of *Selections from Michelangelo Drawings*, including those by O. Zoff, H. Leporini, etc.; of these only the volume by A. E. Popham (London, 1930) is of value for his charming descriptions of twelve drawings.

II. SINGLE PERIODS

11. Friedrich von Portheim, *Beiträge zu den Werken Michelangelos*, in *Repertorium für Kunstwissenschaft*, Vol. XII (1889), p. 140 f. (Contains, *inter alia*, the first attributions of the pen and ink drawings after Giotto and Masaccio to Michelangelo.)

12. Giovanni Morelli, *Handzeichnungen italienischer Meister* . . . , in *Kunstchronik*, new series III (1891–92) and IV (1892–93). (Contradicts von Portheim with regard to the attribution of the early pen and ink drawings to Michelangelo. Discusses the presentation drawings for Perini, etc.)

13. Heinrich Wölfflin, *Die Jugendwerke des Michelangelo*. Munich, 1891. (Discusses on pp. 61 and 85 f. a number of drawings.)

14. Wilhelm Köhler, *Michelangelos Schlachtkarton*, in *Kunsthistorisches Jahrbuch der Zentralkommission*, Vienna, 1907, pp. 115 f. (Discusses the drawings connected with Michelangelo's Battle Cartoon.)

14A. Carl Justi, *Der Carton* (a chapter on the lost Battle Cartoon, in his *Michelangelo, Neue Beiträge zur Erklärung seiner Werke*, pp. 151–172). Berlin, 1909.

15. Aldo Bertini, *Michelangelo fino alla Sistina*, 2nd edition, Turin, 1945.

16. Fritz Baumgart, *Die Jugendzeichnungen Michelangelos bis 1506* in *Marburger Jahrbuch für Kunstwissenschaft*, Vol. X (1937), p. 209 f. Also Separatum of 54 pp., Marburg, 1939. (The best and most consistent discussion of the early drawings.)

17. Charles de Tolnay, *The Youth of Michelangelo*. Princeton, 1947. (With a Catalogue Raisonné of the drawings, of which he himself has published many for the first time.

18. Ernst Steinmann, *Die Sixtinische Kapelle*, Vol. II. Munich, 1905. (A part also separately printed in folio under the title *Die Handzeichnungen Michelangelos*. Munich, n.d.) (Catalogue of drawings, connected with the frescoes, p. 587 f.)

19. Charles de Tolnay, *The Sistine Ceiling*. Princeton, 1945. (With a Catalogue of the drawings.)

20. Anny E. Popp, *Die Medicikapelle Michelangelos*. Munich, 1922.

21. Charles de Tolnay, *The Medici Chapel*. Princeton, 1948. (With a Catalogue of the drawings of about 1519–31, including the presentation drawings for Tommaso de' Cavalieri.)

22. F. Baumgart and B. Biagetti, *Die Fresken des Michelangelo in der Cappella Paolina*. Città del Vaticano, 1934.

III. MICHELANGELO DRAWINGS IN PUBLIC COLLECTIONS

FLORENCE, UFFIZI AND CASA BUONARROTI

23. *Album Michelangiolesco dei disegni originali; riprodotti in fotolitografia.* Florence, 1875.

FLORENCE, UFFIZI

23A. Emil Jacobsen & Nerino Ferri, *Dessins inconnus de Michel-Ange, récemment découverts aux Offices de Florence.* Leipzig, 1905.

FLORENCE, ARCHIVIO BUONARROTI

24. Charles de Tolnay, *Die Handzeichnungen Michelangelos im Archivio Buonarroti*, in *Münchner Jahrbuch der bildenden Kunst*, Vol. V (1928), p. 450 f.

HAARLEM, TEYLER MUSEUM

25. F. van Marcuard, *Die Zeichnungen Michelangelos im Museum Teyler zu Haarlem.* Munich, 1901. (Valuable only for the plates printed by Bruckmann; the notes by van Marcuard are of little use.)

26. Erwin Panofsky, *Bemerkungen zu der Neuherausgabe der Haarlemer Michelangelo-Zeichnungen durch Fr. Knapp* in *Repertorium für Kunstwissenschaft*, Vol. XLVIII, p. 25 f. Berlin, 1927.

26A. Johannes Wilde, *Zur Kritik der Haarlemer Michelangelo-Zeichnungen*, in *Belvedere* XI (1927), Heft 59, p. 142–147.

LONDON, BRITISH MUSEUM

27. Louis Fagan, *The Art of Michael Angelo Buonarroti in the British Museum.* London, 1883. (This volume is out of date. For the drawings in the British Museum one can only use Frey's text volume, Thode VI, and Berenson II, pp. 78–193, 230–232, 322–323. A complete catalogue of the Michelangelo drawings in the B.M. by J. Wilde and A. E. Popham, is in preparation.)

LONDON, BRITISH MUSEUM

28. *Descriptive Catalogue of the Drawings by the Old Masters, forming the Collection of John Malcolm*, by J. C. Robinson. London, 1869.

LONDON, BRITISH MUSEUM

29. *Drawings in the Collection . . . of T. Fitzroy Phillips Fenwick*, by A. E. Popham, London, 1935.

LONDON, BRITISH MUSEUM

30. Wolf Maurenbrecher, *Die Aufzeichnungen des Michelangelo Buonarroti im Britischen Museum*, etc., in *Römische Forschungen der Biblioteca Hertziana*, Vol. XIV. Leipzig, 1938.

LONDON, LAWRENCE COLLECTION

31. *A series of facsimiles of original drawings by M. Angelo Buonarroti selected from the matchless Collection formed by Sir Thomas Lawrence.* London, 1853. (Published by S. and A. Woodburn. The drawings are now in the Ashmolean Museum, the British Museum, the Louvre, and in Haarlem.)

OXFORD

32. *The Drawings by Michel Angelo and Raffaello in the University Galleries, Oxford*, by J. C. Robinson. Oxford, 1870. (With a very good introduction about the history of the drawings, a note on Battista Franco, and reproductions of 84 papermarks.)

OXFORD (*continued*)

32A. Joseph Fisher, *Drawings and Studies in the University Galleries, Oxford.* London, 1879.

33. *Drawings of the Old Masters in the University Galleries and in the Library of Christ Church, Oxford*, by Sidney Colvin. Oxford, 1903–07.

34. *Drawings by the Old Masters in the Library of Christ Church, Oxford*, by C. F. Bell, Oxford, 1914.

PARIS, LOUVRE

35. *Notice des dessins, cartons, pastels . . . au Musée National du Louvre; première partie: Ecole d'Italie*, etc., par Reiset. Paris, 1878.

35A. *Deuxième notice supplémentaire: Dessins, cartons . . . exposés depuis 1879 au Musée National du Louvre*, par Both de Tauzia, Paris, 1888.

36. Louis Demonts, *Les dessins de Michel-Ange* (au Musée du Louvre). Paris, n.d. (1922). (Demonts reproduces eleven drawings which he thinks genuine and five as doubtful. The publication is neither critical nor complete. See No. 50.)
There are two attractive old publications, the one also containing reproductions of a few Michelangelo drawings: '*Recueil de 283 estampes . . . d'après les dessins de grands Maistres, que possedoit autrefois Mr. Jabach.* Paris, Joullein, 1754'. This is actually a reprint of 286 engravings from drawings, issued in six folders between *c.* 1660 and 1670. The other publication on drawings, some by Michelangelo, which are now at the Louvre, is 'P. J. Mariette, *Description sommaire des dessins des grands maistres d'Italie . . . du cabinet de feu M. Crozat.* Paris, 1741'.

VIENNA, ALBERTINA

37. Franz Wickhoff, *Die italienischen Handzeichnungen der Albertina*, in *Jahrbuch der Kunsthistorischen Sammlungen* XII and XIII (Vienna, 1891 and 1892).

38. *Albertina Catalogue III*: Alfred Stix and L. Frölich-Bum, *Beschreibender Katalog der Handzeichnungen in der Albertina: Die toskanischen, umbrischen und römischen Schulen.* Vienna, 1932.

39. *An Exhibition of Old Master Drawings from the Albertina.* (Catalogue by A. E. Popham.) London, 1948.

VIENNA, ALBERTINA

40. Facsimiles: (*a*) *Schönbrunner-Meder*, 12 portfolios, Vienna, 1896–1908; (*b*) *Joseph Meder, new series I.*, Vienna, 1922 (English edition, 1930); (*c*) *Alfred Stix, new series II.*, Vienna, 1925.

WINDSOR CASTLE, ROYAL LIBRARY

41. Johannes Wilde, *The Drawings of Michelangelo and his School, Sebastiano del Piombo, Daniele da Volterra, Baccio Bandinelli and Raffaello da Montelupo* (in A. E. Popham's 'The Italian Drawings of the XV and XVI centuries in the Collection of His Majesty the King at Windsor Castle'). London, 1949. (The most important contribution towards a critical understanding of Michelangelo's drawings as a whole.)

IV. CRITICAL NOTES · ICONOLOGY CHRONOLOGY

42. Otto Hettner, *Zeichnerische Gepflogenheiten bei Michelangelo* in *Monatshefte für Kunstwissenschaft*, Berlin, 1909.

43. (*a*) Franz Wickhoff, *Die Antike im Bildungsgange Michelangelos*, in *Mitteilungen des Instituts für österreichische Geschichtsforschung*. Vienna, 1882.
(*b*) Alois Grünwald, *Über einige Werke Michelangelos und ihr Verhältnis zur Antike*, in *Vienna Yearbook* (Jahrbuch der Kunsthistorischen Sammlungen des Allerhöchsten Kaiserhauses), Vol. 27, part 4, 1908.
(*c*) Anton Hekler, *Michelangelo und die Antike*, in *Wiener Jahrbuch für Kunstgeschichte*, VII, 1930, pp. 201-23.

44. Franz Wickhoff, *Abhandlungen Vorträge und Anzeigen* (herausgegeben von Max Dvořák). Berlin, 1913.

45. Anny E. Popp, *Bemerkungen zu einigen Zeichnungen Michelangelos*, in *Zeitschrift für bildende Kunst*, Vol. LIX (1925-26), p. 134 f. and 169 f.; also in Vol. LXI (1927-28) and Vol. LXII (1928-29).

46. Johannes Wilde, *Eine Studie Michelangelos nach der Antike*, in *Mitteilungen des Kunsthistorischen Instituts in Florenz*, Vol. IV, pp. 41-64. Augsburg, 1932.

47. Erwin Panofsky, *Studies in Iconology*. New York, 1939. (Discusses *inter alia* the presentation drawings for Tommaso de' Cavalieri.)

48. Karl Frey, *Die Dichtungen des Michelagniolo Buonarroti*. Berlin, 1897. (A large number of drawings are described, dated and discussed in the commentary, pp. 281-501. The 'register' at the end of the book contains several documents which can be taken as a basis for the chronology of the drawings.)

49. Henry Thode, *Michelangelos Gedichte* (German translation). Berlin, 1914. (The commentary, pp. 259-279, dealing mainly with the chronology of the poems, also proposes dates for some of the drawings. Thode argues in many cases against the chronology of Frey.)

50. Erwin Panofsky, *Die Michelangelo-Literatur seit 1914*, in *Jahrbuch für Kunstgeschichte*, Vol. I (1921-22), Vienna, 1923. (On col. 23 a review of Demonts' little volume of the Louvre drawings; discusses *passim* several other drawings.)

51. Pietro Toesca, *Michelangelo Buonarroti*, in Enciclopedia Italiana, Vol. XXIII, pp. 165-91. Rome, 1934.

52. Charles de Tolnay, *Michelangelo*, in Thieme-Becker's Künstlerlexikon, Vol. XXIV, Leipzig, 1930.

V. FOLLOWERS OF MICHELANGELO

53. L. Dorez, *Nouvelles Recherches sur Michel-Ange et son entourage*, in *Bibliothéque de l'Ecole des Chartes*, Vols. LXXVII and LXXVIII (1916-17).

54. Hermann Voss, *Die Malerei der Spätrenaissance in Rom and Florenz*, Vol. I, Berlin, 1920. (Chapter V, pp. 111-48, *Das plastische Ideal im Kreise Michelangelos*, with valuable notes on Sebastiano del Piombo, Marcello Venusti, Battista Franco, Daniele da Volterra and Jacopino del Conte.)

55. Anny E. Popp, *Garzoni Michelangelos*, in *Belvedere*, Vol. VIII, p. 6 f. Vienna, 1925.

56. Bernard Berenson, *Andrea di Michelangelo e Antonio Mini*, in *L'Arte*, 1935.

57. Carlo Gamba, *Silvio Cosini* in *Dedalo*, X, pp. 228-54, Milan, 1930.

58. Erwin Panofsky, *Kopie oder Fälschung ? Ein Beitrag zur Kritik einiger Zeichnungen aus der Werkstatt Michelangelos*, in *Zeitschrift für bildende Kunst*, LXI (1927-28), pp. 221-44; LXII (1928-29), pp. 179-83; and A. E. Popp's remarks in Vol. LXII (1928), pp. 54-67.

59. Oskar Fischel, *A new approach to Sebastiano del Piombo as a draughtsman*, in *Old Master Drawings*, 1939-40.

60. Rodolfo Pallucchini, *Sebastian Viniziano* (Fra Sebastiano del Piombo). Milan, 1944. (The Catalogue discusses also the previous attributions of Michelangelo drawings to Sebastiano del Piombo by Wickhoff, d'Achiardi, Berenson, Dussler, etc.)

61. A. Bertolotti, *Don Giulio Clovio*, Modena, 1882. (Recording the Michelangelo drawings in the collection of Giulio Clovio, and his copies after them.)

62. Kurt Kusenberg, *Le Rosso*. Paris, 1931. (Proves that several drawings which Berenson attributed to Michelangelo are by Rosso Fiorentino.)

63. F. Baumgart, *Daniele da Volterra e Michelangelo* in *Bollettino d'Arte*, XXVIII, 1934. (Other attributions of drawings to Daniele da Volterra by E. Panofsky in *Festschrift für J. Schlosser*, Vienna, 1927.)

Correction to p. 43, footnote 70. The 1871 edition of Starkey's writings was edited by J. M. Cowper, the 1948 edition of the 'Dialogue' by Kathleen Burton.

INDEX OF COLLECTIONS